David Taylor

111 Places
in Newcastle
That You
Shouldn't Miss

T0150546

emons:

Did you enjoy this guidebook? Would you like to see more?
Join us in uncovering new places around the world on:
www.111places.com

Foreword

Newcastle and Gateshead face each other across the River Tyne. Two separate towns, they are now often joined together for marketing purposes as NewcastleGateshead. Cooperation is a fine thing, but good-natured – and occasionally fractious – competition over the centuries has given both a unique character.

Tyneside has always been a busy and dynamic place. Once it was shipbuilding and coal that drove the local economy. These industries have long gone, but others have since sprung up in their place. Now a typical working day is more likely to involve a PC and an internet connection than heavy machinery. The creative arts have strong roots in both Newcastle and Gateshead too. Newcastle is the home of *Viz* and the birthplace of Sting. Gateshead can boast a world-class live music venue in the Sage, and in the BALTIC, possibly the quirkiest contemporary fine art gallery in the country.

Newcastle has a reputation as a party town. You don't have to walk very far down one of its streets before coming across a pub or a restaurant. At the weekend, there are always crowds of young lads and lasses out in the city having a good time – and in the skimpiest of clothing, even in winter.

Another frequent comment made about Geordies is how warm and friendly they are. If you want to make a new friend just go and stand in a bus queue. Throw in a few pithy comments about how the Toon did that weekend and you'll have a friend for life. Just don't say that they're gannin doon. Unless they look like a Sunderland supporter.

What has been so wonderful about writing this book is that it's helped me see both Newcastle and Gateshead with new eyes. I've also discovered new aspects of both towns that I'd not previously been aware of – how I got this far without visiting the Lit & Phil I'll never know. I hope you have as much fun exploring the places in this book as I had writing about them.

111 Places

1__9 Carlton Terrace

All the lads and lasses there...

Reality TV is now a permanent fixture on our television screens. One of the most popular and long-lived of these shows is MTV's *Geordie Shore*, filmed on Tyneside and first shown in 2011. The show is modelled on *Jersey Shore*, which ran for three years from 2009 and was filmed in New Jersey, USA. *Geordie Shore* has long outlasted its predecessor and continues to be broadcast, with its 21st series airing in 2020.

The premise of the show is simple: a small group of twenty-somethings, a mix of male and female, live together in a house for a period of a month. Cameras follow their glamorous, and often hedonistic lives during that month, both in the house and around Newcastle. All of the housemates are from north-east England, and many have since become stars in their own right.

The first series of *Geordie Shore* was shot in 9 Carlton Terrace in the prosperous suburb of Jesmond, the five-bedroom Victorian town house converted to make it suitable for shooting a television production. What the other residents of this quiet late-Victorian terrace thought about this was sadly never noted. Fortunately, further disruption was avoided the following year when the 'house' for the second series was created in a converted warehouse on an industrial estate in Wallsend. Since then, with the exception of four series made abroad, every episode of *Geordie Shore* has been recorded in this more controlled setting.

It has to be said that *Geordie Shore* isn't for everyone; it is far from high art. The show has been accused of being borderline pornography, and questions have even been raised in Parliament about the stars' onscreen consumption of alcohol. However, there is no such thing as bad publicity; after the transmission of the first series, Newcastle benefited from an increase in visitor numbers. As for 9 Carlton Terrace, it has now returned to private domestic calm.

Address 9 Carlton Terrace, Jesmond Road West, Newcastle, NE2 4PD | **Getting there** Bus 1, 33A, 38 and various others to Sandyford Road–Civic Centre | **Hours** Viewable from the outside only | **Tip** The Holy Hobo, an atmospheric lounge bar and restaurant, is just a 5-minute walk from Carlton Terrace (Jesmond Three Sixty, Jesmond, NE2 1DB, www.holyhobo.co.uk).

2 Al-Azhar Mosque

From the Middle East to North East

The Al-Azhar Mosque in South Shields is the region's oldest purpose-built mosque. Serving the Islamic Yemeni community of South Tyneside, the mosque is a symbol of the peaceful integration of immigrants into Britain.

In 1839, Aden, now in the Republic of Yemen, was acquired by the British East India Company. Thanks to its position on the Red Sea, Aden became an important resupply point for ships sailing between Britain and her territorial possessions in the Indian Ocean. Yemeni sailors found work on British merchant ships, often doing the hot and dirty job of stoking. They were first officially recorded as a presence in South Shields in the 1860s. In 1894, the first boarding house solely for the use of Yemeni and Arab sailors was opened. Gradually more boarding houses and Arab businesses opened in the town, run by Yemenis who made the decision to stay on Tyneside.

The Yemeni settlers initially worshipped in converted buildings in South Shields. These were known as Zaoia, or 'corner', as the buildings were often on street corners. The first Zaoia was on Cuthbert Street, opposite the Lord Clyde pub. This Zaoia was closed when Cuthbert Street was swallowed up by the building of the Western Approach. The need for a more permanent place of worship eventually resulted in the opening of the purpose-built Al-Azhar Mosque in 1971.

The Yemeni are now indelibly woven into the life of South Shields, often through the marriage of Yemeni men to local women. Now there are thought to be fifth – even sixth – generation Yemeni living in the town. Fittingly, it was in connection with marriage that the Al-Azhar Mosque had its most notable event. During a busy visit to South Shields in July 1977, Muhammad Ali had his recent marriage to Veronica Porsche blessed at the mosque. Over 7,000 crowded the streets to see the boxer, with a lucky 300 witnessing the blessing inside.

Address Laygate, South Shields, NE33 5RP | Getting there Bus T 503 to
B1301-Commercial Road; Metro to South Shields (Yellow Line), then a 20-minute
walk; on-street parking on Laygate | Hours Not generally open to the public other than
as a place of worship | Tip The Temple Memorial Park is a large open recreational space
six minutes' drive from the Al-Azhar Mosque. Named after Archbishop William Temple,
the park was gifted to South Tyneside in 1946 by the Ecclesiastical Commissioners in
recognition of the region's role during World War II.

3 Alderman Fenwick's House
A Dickens of a history

Formerly known as Numbers 98/100 Pilgrim Street, Alderman Fenwick's House is one of the oldest brick buildings in Newcastle. Built in the 1670s, the first owner was Thomas Winship, who was a member of the Tanners' Company. When Thomas died in September 1695 the property passed to his daughter Sarah, who was by then married to Nicholas Fenwick, the scion of a successful merchant family from Newcastle. It was during their joint ownership of the house that a number of alterations were made. This included the addition of a decorative ceiling to the building's 'Great Room', as well as the creation of the Oak Stair that led up and into a lantern tower with panoramic views across the city. The reason that Fenwick is associated with the building, and not Winship, is largely due to an attribution on a 1723 map of Newcastle by James Corbridge.

Ownership of the building passed to a Thomas Carr who, in 1781, sold it on to Charles Turner. Turner converted the house into a coaching inn named The Queen's Head Inn, proudly advertising it as being 'fitted in a genteel manner'. For just over a century the inn was a popular stop on the Great North Road between London and Edinburgh. One guest was the author Charles Dickens, who, during a five-day stay in 1861, rakishly ran up an extravagant bill of £36!

In 1883, the building lease was taken on by the Newcastle upon Tyne Liberal Club, which stayed until 1962. At this point the fortunes of the building took a downward turn. Largely abandoned, the structure became increasingly shabby and derelict, with demolition threatened at one point. Fortunately, good sense prevailed and the building was saved by Newcastle City Council. By 1997, under the care of the Tyne and Wear Building Preservation Trust, the building was fully restored to its former glory, and it is now leased to local businesses as office space. Alderman Fenwick would surely approve of that.

Address 98/100 Pilgrim Street, Newcastle, NE1 6SQ, central-space.co.uk | Getting there Bus 53 Voltra, X24, X24A or X34 to Pilgrim Street; paid parking at NCP Carliol Square | Hours Not generally open to the public, but internal viewings can be arranged through Central Space by ringing +44 (0)191 644 4039 | Tip The nearby Market Lane pub is locally known as the Monkey Bar. The nickname dates from the 19th century when Irish bricklayers, employed in the redevelopment of the city centre, would use their hods – or monkeys – as security against their drinks bill.

4 All Saints' Church

The church on the hill

The graceful Georgian spire of All Saints' Church in Newcastle is a prominent landmark on the quayside. It is one of the four original parish churches of Newcastle, and yet, until relatively recently, was largely abandoned.

All Saints' Church stands on the site of an earlier 13th-century church. This church, built in the Gothic style, was completely demolished to build All Saints'. Largely in poor repair, with some parts in danger of collapse, the steeple of the old church still required the use of gunpowder to bring it down. This resulted in the death of Captain William Hedley who, having stepped through the great west door at the wrong moment, was struck on the head by falling stones. This 'instantly deprived him of sense, and, in a few hours, of life'.

Designed by local architect David Stephenson, All Saints' was completed in 1789 at the cost of £27,000 – equivalent to approximately £2.3 million today. The design of the church has a number of notable features. The exterior is in the neoclassical style common for the time, but All Saints' is the only church in England with an elliptical nave. Mahogany and decorative plasterwork dominate the interior, where there is seating for 1,300 people.

For the first 160 years, All Saints' was well used by churchgoers. However, by the late 1950s attendance was below the numbers necessary to justify use of the building. In 1961, All Saints' was deconsecrated, and converted to office space. In the 1990s it was the temporary rehearsal space for the Northern Sinfonia until the opening of Sage Gateshead in 2004 (see ch. 75). Flooding in 2009 caused extensive damage, and in 2015 All Saints' found its way onto Historic England's Heritage at Risk register. Happily, since then an extensive restoration project has rescued the church, with a lease awarded to the Evangelical Presbyterian Church to hold services there once again.

Address Pilgrim Street, Newcastle, NE1 3HA | Getting there Bus Q1/Q3 Quaylink to Quayside Guildhall; paid parking at Quayside Multi Storey Car Park | Hours Viewable from the outside only | Tip The nearby Holy Jesus Hospital was built in 1681. The building is one of Newcastle's two 17th-century brick buildings, the other being Alderman Fenwick's House (see ch. 3). Closed to the public, the building is now a National Trust office building.

5   Angel of the North Model
An icon in miniature

Art doesn't have to be exclusive. Perched high above the A1 on the site of an old pithead, the *Angel of the North* is the UK's most viewed sculpture. It has been calculated that on average the *Angel* is seen by one person every second. The *Angel*'s visibility is largely a result of its impressive size. Consider these statistics: the *Angel* is 66 feet tall with a wingspan of 177 feet (often erroneously said to be larger than a Jumbo Jet – it's big but not *that* big). And, the *Angel* is 200 tonnes of corten steel which, thanks to the 600 tonne concrete foundations, can withstand the force of a 100mph wind.

The *Angel of the North*, designed by the artist Antony Gormley, was erected in 1998. However, Gormley began with a 1/20 scale model to test out his design and convince Gateshead Council leaders of the sculpture's viability. Having achieved those aims, the model is now fittingly on display in the Shipley Art Gallery. Made from balsa wood and plaster, the model has been painted to match the distinctive ruddy brown of the real thing. At this smaller scale, it's far easier to appreciate the finer details of the design, such as the way that the structural ribs flow sinuously up and around the *Angel*'s body, which, like many of Gormley's figurative pieces, was based on his own body.

Gormley's wooden model was used to create a series of 12 limited-edition *Angel*s cast in bronze and signed by the artist. In 2008, one of the statuettes had a starring role on the BBC's *Antiques Road-show* when the show was broadcast from Gateshead. Appraised by expert Philip Mould, the model was valued at £1 million and was the first object featured on the show to hit that magical valuation figure. Then, in 2011 another version of the model was sold at Sotheby's for £3.4 million, doubling the expected sale price and more than four times the original cost of the full-size version. Fortunately, the real thing is free to view anytime you like.

Address Shipley Art Gallery, Prince Consort Road, Gateshead, NE8 4JB | Getting there
Bus Q2 Quaylink, S844 to Prince Consort Road–Shipcote Lane, or bus 21 Angel, 25 or
28B to Durham Road–Northbourne Street; Metro to Gateshead (Yellow or Green Line),
then a 16-minute walk; free parking to a maximum of 3 hours at Prince Consort Road Car
Park | Tip The *Angel of the North* is free to visit all year round, with space for 26 cars in a
nearby car park on the A167.

6 _ BALTIC
From flour to fine art

BALTIC on the Gateshead quayside is one of Britain's foremost contemporary art galleries. There is no permanent collection on show, but a rolling programme of exhibitions ensures that there is something for everyone to enjoy across its four galleries.

Notable names who have exhibited at BALTIC include Yoko Ono, Antony Gormley and Spencer Tunick. In 2005, Tunick managed the impressive feat of persuading 2,000 people to strip off for a series of group photos on the quayside, photos that were then shown at BALTIC. In 2011, BALTIC played host to the annual Turner Prize, the first time a gallery outside London or Liverpool had done so since the first Turner Prize award in 1984.

Possibly the most striking thing about BALTIC, however, is the building itself. You do not have to look too hard to see the words *Baltic Flour Mills* emblazoned across the north face, or *Joseph Rank Limited* on the south. The building is the sole survivor of a number of mills that once stood on the Tyne. Commissioned by Rank Hovis and opened in 1950, the Baltic Flour Mill was a thoroughly modern and efficient mill at the time, even though the design was drawn up in the 1930s. Strangely, there is no agreement on why the mill was named Baltic. Other Rank Hovis mills in the country were named after seas or rivers, so the mill may have been named after the Baltic Sea. However, it may also be named after the Baltic Exchange in London, once the centre of wheat trading in Britain. The mill closed in 1981 and stood empty for a number of years until, after extensive and expensive conversion work, BALTIC opened in 2002.

The name of Joseph Rank is a fitting one to be associated with a centre for art. In the 1930s, J. Arthur Rank, one of Rank's sons, invested money from the flour business in British film production. This led to the making of classic movies such as *Henry V* and *A Matter of Life and Death*.

Address Gateshead Quays, South Shore Road, Gateshead, NE8 3BA, +44 (0)191 478 1810, baltic.art | Getting there Bus Q2 Quaylink to Baltic Square; paid parking at South Shore Road Car Park and Mill Road Car Park | Hours Daily 10am–6pm | Tip Gateshead Riverside Park above Pipewellgate offers a pleasant walk along the Tyne towards Dunston. The park was developed as an open-air art venue with a number of modern sculptures to be seen within its grounds.

7 Bessie Surtees House

Newcastle's Romeo and Juliet elope down a ladder

It is 18 November, 1772, late on a dark, moonless night. Two men scurry through the quiet streets of Newcastle carrying a ladder between them. They come to 41 Sandhill, a handsome timber-framed building and home of the banker Aubone Surtees. Furtively the ladder is raised to a first floor window. Heart thumping, John Scott climbs the ladder to tap softly on the glass. Bessie – Aubone's daughter – opens the window and gently kisses his face. She climbs out and John lovingly helps her to the ground. They briefly embrace, for there is no time to be lost; they are to flee to the Scottish Borders, where they can be married against their families' wishes. John thanks his friend and the couple slip away. The friend looks at the ladder. Scratching his head, he wonders how to return it now he is alone.

Although the fine details of John and Bessie's elopement are a little fuzzy more than two centuries on – the friend's name is not recorded, though he definitely had a ladder – what *is* known is that both families eventually forgave the couple, who had a long and happy marriage. John was the son of a coal merchant. Educated at the Royal Grammar School, he had a reputation for being an unwilling pupil prone to practical jokes. Despite this, after completing his studies at Oxford, he practised law before becoming a Member of Parliament. In 1801 he was appointed Lord Chancellor, a role he held for five years.

Now known as Bessie Surtees House, no. 41 Sandhill still stands, though with busy pubs nearby the nights are no longer quiet. The building is the regional headquarters of Historic England. Most of it is used as office space, but the first floor is open to the public. There can be seen a reproduction of a typical Jacobean interior, as well as an exhibition detailing the history of the house and the elopement. Leaving by the window is no longer encouraged, however. Nor, come to that, is bringing a ladder with you when you visit.

Address 41–44 Sandhill, Newcastle, NE1 3JF, +44 (0)191 269 1255 | Getting there Bus Q1/Q3 Quaylink to Quayside Guildhall; paid parking at Close/Swing Bridge Car Park | Hours Mon–Fri 10am–4pm, closed on bank holidays | Tip Bessie Surtees House is not the only Jacobean building on Newcastle's Quayside. The nearby Redhouse pub building, where you can find a wide range of traditional pies, is a similar age.

8 Billy
Railway mania

Imagine discovering that you're 10 years older than you'd previously been led to believe. That wouldn't normally be a cause for celebration. This is not the case for *Billy*, a steam locomotive on permanent display at Stephenson Steam Railway. *Billy* was built in the West Moor workshops at Killingworth Colliery, under the watchful eye of railway pioneer George Stephenson. *Billy*'s role wasn't glamorous; the engine spent its working life pulling waggons from the colliery to the River Tyne.

Until recently *Billy* was thought to have been built in 1826, just a few years before Stephenson's more famous locomotive *Rocket*. Research in 2018 upended that belief and pushed *Billy*'s construction date back to 1816. Although none of *Billy*'s components are now original, the design and features of *Billy* convinced experts that the earlier date was correct. This means that *Billy* has now jumped up to third place in the list of the oldest surviving locomotives in the world. *Billy* does have one important distinction though: it *is* now the oldest surviving standard gauge steam engine. Gauge is the distance between the tracks that a train runs along. *Billy* has a gauge of 4 foot 8½ inches, just like almost all modern passenger trains.

Stephenson was born in 1781 in Wylam to poor parents, neither of whom could read or write. Remarkably, the small cottage where Stephenson was born still stands and can be seen from the Wylam Waggonway path. There was no money to send young George to school. It was only when he was earning money – as an engineman at a pit in Newburn – that he was able to pay for lessons at a night school. Despite this early lack of education, Stephenson had a natural aptitude for engineering. *Billy* was just one triumph in a lifetime of achievement. It's therefore a pity that he's not around now to see how far railways have spread around the world. He'd surely be chuffed.

Address Stephenson Steam Railway, Middle Engine Lane, North Shields, NE29 8DX, +44 (0)191 277 7135, www.stephensonsteamrailway.org.uk | **Getting there** Bus 91, 310 Cobalt & Coast, 335 to Middle Engine Lane Cobalt South; free on-site parking | **Hours** Sat & Sun between Easter and the end of October, daily during school holidays, and bank holidays, all 11am–4pm | **Tip** Stephenson lived at Dial Cottage while working on steam engines for the Killingworth Colliery. This cottage is also still standing and can be seen on the Great Lime Road in Forest Hall.

9 Black Gate

Halt! Who goes there?

At first glance, Black Gate looks... superfluous. It is a medieval gatehouse to nowhere, with nothing on either side to stop you sneaking around (though be careful not to fall into the deep ditch below the south wall). The clue to its original purpose is the nearby Keep, now separated from Black Gate by the East Coast Main Line. Built between 1247 and 1250, Black Gate was the northern entrance in the walls surrounding the Keep. These walls are largely long gone, with only a few scant remnants surviving. However, one reminder that Black Gate was once next to an enclosed space is Castle Garth, the name of the area south of the gatehouse. This was an area within the castle walls, garth being a medieval word for yard.

Originally, Black Gate would have had a drawbridge and portcullis. It would also have been far less tall than it currently is. Its height was initially increased by Alexander Stephenson, who leased the gatehouse from King James I in 1618. After having had the builders in, Stephenson leased Black Gate to a London merchant named Patrick Black. Further work was carried out by John Pickell, who left his name and the year, 1636, on a stone high up on the south wall.

By the 19th century, the Black Gate area of Newcastle was one of the poorest in the city. Black Gate was used as slum housing with 60 people living there at one point. Ultimately, it was the Society of Antiquaries of Newcastle upon Tyne that rescued the building, taking it over in 1883. The society replaced what would have been a flat roof with the jaunty pitched one Black Gate currently sports.

There are several theories as to why the gatehouse is known as Black Gate. The most likely is that it is named after Stephenson's tenant. However, more grisly theories have also been put forward, including one that the colour refers to the blood from those squashed by the portcullis as it was lowered.

Address Castle Garth, Newcastle, NE1 1RQ, +44 (0)191 230 6300, www.newcastlecastle.co.uk | **Getting there** Bus 27 Crusader, 56 Cityrider, 57 Citylink, 58 Citylink and various others to High Level Bridge North End | **Hours** Viewable from the outside only | **Tip** Black Gate is just a 2-minute walk away from El Torero, an authentic Spanish restaurant selling tapas and speciality dishes (Milburn House, Side City Centre, Newcastle, NE1 1PR, eltorero.co.uk).

10 Blackfriars

Living the cloistered life

Newcastle United is famous for its black and white football strip. However, the Toon were not the first Novocastrians to wear these colours. The Order of Preachers, informally known as the Dominicans, is a Roman Catholic mendicant order, committed to a life of poverty, prayer and contemplation. Founded in France by St Dominic in 1216, the order arrived in England in 1221. Once established in the country they were known as Blackfriars due to the black *cappa* or cloak worn over their white tunics.

The area now known as Blackfriars was acquired by the order in 1239, the land donated by three pious sisters. The first buildings were lost in a fire of 1248, but were rebuilt by 1250 and are those still standing now. Blackfriars is one of the oldest buildings in Newcastle and is the only medieval friary extant in the city.

The Blackfriars themselves are long gone. The end came in 1539 with Henry VIII's dissolution of the monasteries in England. After its acquisition by the Crown, the church in the friary grounds was demolished, and the land sold to the Newcastle Corporation for £53, 7 shillings and 6 pence. The remaining buildings were then divided up and leased to nine of the town's crafts guilds, who used them as a meeting place four times a year.

By the 1960s, Blackfriars was in danger of demolition. By then the buildings had suffered almost a century of neglect. In 1931, the Saddlers' property had been condemned as being unfit for human habitation, and a newspaper article of 1951 described Blackfriars as 'decrepit … dilapidated'. It was Peter Renwick, Mayor of Newcastle in 1963 and 1964, who ultimately saved Blackfriars. Renwick pushed for its rescue and so, in 1973, extensive restoration began. Since then, Blackfriars has been used by a variety of businesses. It is now home to Blackfriars Restaurant, which serves food that might tempt even the most devout.

Address Friars Street, Newcastle, NE1 4XN, +44 (0)191 261 5945, www.blackfriarsrestaurant.co.uk | **Getting there** Bus 131, 685, X82 or X85 to Newcastle St James (Stand D); Metro to St James (Yellow Line); paid parking at The Gate Car Park | **Hours** Mon–Sat noon–2.30pm & 5.30–9.45pm, Sun noon–4pm; booking essential | **Tip** Just 5-minutes' walk from Blackfriars, The Gate is a modern shopping centre with a multi-screen cinema and wide range of restaurants, conveniently placed for a post-movie meal (www.thegatenewcastle.co.uk).

11 By The River Brew Co.

Been around the world...

The invention of the shipping container revolutionised how manufactured goods are transported around the world. Roughly 95 per cent of exported goods are sent by sea and – with few exceptions – they will have been stored in a shipping container during the journey. A regular-sized shipping container is a simple thing: essentially just a huge metal box that can hold – and someone has taken the time to calculate this – 8,000 shoe boxes.

Shipping containers can be stacked, one on top of another, allowing huge numbers to be crammed onto the decks of cargo ships. The logistics of loading and unloading thousands of shipping containers every day led to the demise of old docks and ports, built when loose cargo was laboriously unloaded by crane. The River Tyne was just one river where this change took place. Now, goods arrive and depart from the huge Tyne Container Terminal near Jarrow, rather than Newcastle or Gateshead.

A few shipping containers have made their way upriver, however. By The River Brew Co. is a new £1.5-million development under the Tyne Bridge in Gateshead, where the 1980s nightclub *Tuxedo Princess* was once moored. The community of businesses that occupy the site are housed in recycled shipping containers. It's a very geometric and industrial aesthetic, but the By The River Brew Co. still feels welcoming despite this. What's on offer largely depends on the season. There are permanent establishments such as the Brewery & Tap Room, and Träkol with its open fire kitchen. If you need your bike servicing then the Backyard Bike Shop is a must. While you wait, you can order coffee or even discuss the building of a custom bike, tailored to your specific needs. From spring to autumn the Hawker Market is open, with independent traders selling a wide range of street food and goods. But the best thing about it all? You don't have to cross several oceans to find it.

Address Hillgate Quays, Gateshead, NE8 2FD, +44 (0)191 737 1120, www.bytheriverbrew.co |
Getting there Bus Q1 Quaylink to Hillgate Quay; Metro to Gateshead (Yellow or Green
Line), then a 9-minute walk; paid parking at South Shore Road Car Park and Mill Road Car
Park | **Hours** Mon–Thu noon–11pm, Fri & Sat noon–11.45pm, Sun noon–10pm | **Tip**
Newcastle also has a shipping container community. The Stack on Pilgrim Street is an eclectic
collection of shops, eateries and bars, arranged around a central courtyard used for live events.

12 Byker Wall

Colourful modernism

The reputation of post-war British architecture has never been lower. Criticised for its inhuman design aesthetic, the architecture of the 1950s, 1960s and 1970s is now largely seen as a blight on the country's towns and cities. One of the building materials commonly used post-war was concrete. It was cheap and easy to use, but with an austere visual quality that lacks the cheerful character of brick or wood.

One architectural project of the period that bucks the Brutalist trend is the Byker Wall. Post-war, Byker was a town of 17,000 people who lived in Victorian back-to-back terraces. It was a poor, working-class but tight-knit community. By the 1960s, the housing was considered unfit for human habitation by city planners, with many homes lacking bathrooms. A decision was made to redevelop Byker completely, to knock down the terraces but to keep the community intact. Ralph Erskine, the architect in charge of the project, stated that 'the main concern will be for those who are already resident in Byker, and the need to rehouse them without breaking family ties and other valued associations or patterns of life'. During the planning process, residents worked with Erskine, who also had a drop-in centre in Byker.

The result was the Byker Wall, a long ribbon of 620 maisonettes enclosing a housing estate, completed in 1982. The outer wall has relatively few windows, to protect the residents from the noise of a planned motorway that was ultimately never built. The inner wall is a riot of colour, with painted timber and plastics used to decorate surfaces, and has been described as Functionalist Romantic styling.

Has the Byker Wall been a success? Only 20 per cent of the former residents of Byker were ultimately housed in the new development. But establishment of the Byker Community Trust in 2011 is proof that a communal spirit is still important to those who live there.

Address Byker, Newcastle, NE6 | **Getting there** Bus 12, 18 or 18A to Conyers Road or Dalston Street–Dalston Crescent; Metro to Byker (Yellow Line) | **Hours** Viewable from the outside only | **Tip** Climb Newcastle is a rock-climbing gym in the old Byker Swimming Pool building. Climbing routes range from those suitable for beginners to more advanced climbers (Shipley Walk, Byker, NE6 2DQ, +44 (0)191 276 2174, www.climbnewcastle.com).

13   Central Arcade

Shopping in style

There is much fine architecture in Newcastle, and there are many great places to shop. But nowhere are the two brought together in such exuberant style as the Central Arcade in the city's Central Exchange Building.

Designed by John Wardle and George Walker for Richard Grainger, the Central Exchange Building was completed in 1838. Originally intended as the site of Newcastle's corn market, the building was first used as a subscription newsroom. There, for the annual payment of one guinea, members could read the latest newspapers and periodicals. From 1870, the building was used as an art gallery, and then, in 1897, as a vaudeville theatre. The curtain came down on this venture when, in 1901, a fire broke out and destroyed the interior of the building.

This could have been the end of the Central Exchange Building. Instead, the interior was refashioned by the architects Joseph Oswald and Son and, in 1906, reopened as the Central Arcade and Central Exchange Hotel.

An arcade is a covered avenue of shops along which customers can walk, free from the tedious problems of noise, rain and traffic found on city streets. The building of arcades peaked in the late-Victorian and early-Edwardian periods, largely due to the ready availability of cast and wrought iron. Today, of course, we build shopping malls, which achieve the same effect as an arcade with arguably a fraction of the charm.

And the Central Arcade truly is charming. It is light and airy, thanks to the glass barrel-vaulted roof that stretches along its length. On the walls are decorative honey-coloured faience tiles produced by Burmantofts Pottery of Yorkshire. Even the floor is a work of art, a terrazzo mosaic of classical motifs. The shops in the arcade aren't the usual chain stores either; independent boutiques and eateries predominate. All in all, it knocks a modern shopping mall into an Edwardian cocked hat.

Address Market Street, Newcastle, NE1 5BP | Getting there Bus 1, 22 or 22X to Monument Market Street; Metro to Monument (Yellow or Green Line) | Hours Open all year round, though individual shops in the arcade have their own opening and closing times | Tip The Central Arcade has been home to J.G. Windows – Newcastle's oldest music shop – since 1908. Windows sells a wide range of music-related products, from sheet music to the latest audio-visual equipment (jgwindows.com).

14 Centre for Life

Unravelling the secrets of life

The International Centre for Life is a compact science 'village' in the west end of Newcastle. Nearly 600 people from 35 countries currently work there, including research scientists and medical experts, as well as specialists involved in the fields of education and public engagement. Since opening in 2000, life scientists have tackled subjects linked to genetics and regenerative medicine, leading to direct benefits for hundreds of thousands of people in the UK and beyond.

The Centre for Life is home to Newcastle University's Institute of Genetic Medicine. In the past two decades, the institute has gained an enviable international reputation for research into many areas of the life sciences. One notable success story has been the tackling of kidney disease resulting from a brain disorder known as Joubert syndrome. Researchers have developed techniques to use a small strand of engineered DNA to sidestep the genetic mutation that causes the kidney damage.

The Centre for Life is a charity, with the money needed to run the facility entirely self-generated. One of the quirkier ways income is created is with an outdoor ice rink set up in the Centre's grounds over the winter months!

Arguably the most important aspect of the Centre for Life is the promotion of the wonders of science to the general public. This is done through active engagement online and through social media, as well as at the Life Science Centre in the grounds of the Centre for Life. Here you can take a virtual trip into the Universe in the Space Zone, or explore the mind-boggling miracles of the human brain in the Brain Zone. Children can also experiment with real chemicals and scientific equipment in the Chemistry Zone, under supervision. The Life Science Centre also hosts temporary science and technology-related exhibitions, all with the aim of inspiring the next generation of scientists.

Address Times Square, Newcastle, NE1 4EP, +44 (0) 191 243 8210, www.life.org.uk |
Getting there Bus 54 Saltwell Park, 97 Green Arrow, X 30 or X 97 Green Arrow to Central
Station Neville Street (Stand E); Metro to Central Station (Yellow or Green Line); paid
parking at Blandford Square Public Car Park | **Hours** Daily 9.45am–5pm | **Tip** Never
Give Up is a new adventure experience on Scotswood Road in which you have to use your
mental and physical abilities to navigate through a maze and on to a themed escape room
(nevergiveupescape.co.uk).

15 The Chares

Secret passages

The Romans weren't stupid. Even the Normans had their moments. Newcastle is the city it is because the Tyne Valley rises steeply upwards, making it a perfect place to defend. This is handy if the natives are hostile, or if you fear invasion from the unwashed hordes further north. The practical upshot of the city's geography is that you always face an uphill walk from the quayside into the centre of town. Nowhere is this more apparent than if you take a stroll up from the quayside along a chare.

The word 'chare' is peculiar to the north east and refers to a narrow street or alleyway. Newcastle's chares, of which there were once 20, all date from the medieval period. However, many of these were lost during the Great Fire of Newcastle and Gateshead, and were not reinstated. Some of these lost chares had vaguely sinister names, such as Dark Chare which, in 1827, was described by Eneas Mackenzie as so narrow that 'it is very properly termed the Dark Chare, for the houses at the top nearly touch each other'. Only Breakneck Stairs, which links Close and Hanover Street, has a creepier name.

Not all the chares are narrow or particularly steep. Broad Chare, leading to Pandon, is a wide road not an alley. Even in the 1820s, Mackenzie noted, the chare was 'broad enough to admit a cart'. Other chares, such as Cox Chare, were widened after the Great Fire, or replaced by more modern roads, such as Lombard Street near the Tyne Bridge.

If you want a real sense of what a medieval chare was like then you need to climb Castle Stairs. This steep flight of steps gradually winds its way uphill, through the Postern, a doorway in the old town wall, and on to Castle Garth and the Castle. Before you catch your breath, try to imagine that you're now facing grim-faced Normans armed to the hilt and ready to defend their property. It'll help you appreciate just how useful a hill can be.

Address Castle Stairs, Close, Newcastle, NE1 3RE | **Getting there** Bus Q1/Q3 Quaylink to Quayside Guildhall; paid parking at Close Swing Bridge Car Park | **Tip** Tiger Hornsby, at the foot of Castle Stairs, is an award-winning cocktail bar with a constantly changing drinks menu (8–10 Close, Newcastle, NE1 3RE, +44 (0)191 261 6141, tigerhornsby.co.uk).

16 Chimney Mill

A Georgian rooftop ornament

Drive down Claremont Road and be prepared to do a double-take. Sitting on the roof of an otherwise ordinary town house is the octagonal wooden structure of an 18th-century windmill, minus its sails.

The windmill was designed by John Smeaton, who was one of the 18th century's many overachievers. A civil engineer and member of the Royal Society, he pioneered the use of hydraulic lime – a type of mortar that usefully sets under water. This invention enabled Smeaton to successfully build the third Eddystone lighthouse, which lasted for nearly 120 years and was only decommissioned when the rock on which it stood began dangerously to erode. (Dismantled, the lighthouse was moved to Plymouth Hoe, where, known as Smeaton's Tower, it still stands today.)

Smeaton was also associated with the Lunar Society, a group of learned men that included the likes of Erasmus Darwin, grandfather of Charles, and Joseph Priestley, discoverer of oxygen. Smeaton's interest in science led him to experiment with a force pump to keep a diving bell oxygenated. The bell was built to help in the construction of Hexham Bridge, which Smeaton also designed. The new bridge was necessary after the old one was washed away in the Great Flood of 1771, the same flood that destroyed the medieval bridge between Newcastle and Gateshead (see ch. 90).

Given his many interests, it may seem odd that Smeaton would be involved in such a small-scale project as a windmill. However, he had a fascination with waterwheels and windmills, winning the Copley Medal for pioneering research into improving their efficiency. This research had unexpected effects. An experimental paper written by Smeaton resulted in the Smeaton coefficient, an equation used by the Wright Brothers to successfully develop the first powered aircraft in 1903. As for Chimney Mill, it stopped operating in 1891, and its sails were removed in 1924.

Address Claremont Road, Newcastle, NE2 4AL | Getting there Bus 10, 11, X 47 or X 77 and various others to Claremont Road – Claremont Place; paid parking at Claremont Road Car Park | Hours Viewable from the outside only | Tip Chimney Mills is only a 10-minute walk from the offices of BBC Newcastle on Barrack Road. Regular tours are scheduled at the studio, where you can see behind the scenes of a modern television station.

17__Chinatown

A taste of the East

It was shipbuilding that created the first link between Newcastle and China. In 1880, the keel for the cruiser *Yang Wei* was laid down at the Armstrong Whitworth shipyard at Elswick, the first of four ships commissioned by the Chinese Navy. Nearby, in the cemetery of St John's Church, is the 1881 grave of a Chinese sailor, who died of tuberculosis. Although it was unplanned, he was the first Chinese national to make Tyneside his permanent home.

Over the 20th century, the number of Chinese who came and stayed on Tyneside slowly grew. Now there are more than 35,000 Chinese in Newcastle and its suburbs, many of whom are students from China and Hong Kong. The most visible symbol of their presence in the city is Stowell Street, known as Chinatown. The street was once home to the Co-operative Society Banana Ripening Warehouse. This red-brick building still stands and can be recognised by the 'Labor and Wait' motto carved into a decorative frieze near the roofline. Now it hosts a selection of the many restaurants and Chinese shops that run the length of the street.

The first Chinese restaurant in Newcastle was the Marlborough Café on Scotswood Road, which opened in 1949. It was only in 1978 that the first Chinese business, the Wing Hong supermarket, opened on Stowell Street. In the 1970s, Stowell Street was decaying and essentially abandoned. This soon changed as other Chinese businesses moved there too, including restaurants such as the King Neptune – which, like the Wing Hong supermarket, is still trading today.

The magnificent 36-foot-tall Chinese arch that welcomes visitors to Chinatown was erected in 2004. Built by craftsmen from Shanghai, the arch may seem authentically Chinese. Look closely though and you can see decorative panels that show scenes from northern life. Fittingly, one of these panels shows shipyard cranes, bringing the story full circle.

Address Stowell Street, Newcastle, NE1 4XQ | Getting there Bus 131, 685, X 82 or
X 85 to Newcastle St James (Stand D); Metro to St James (Yellow Line); paid parking at
The Gate Car Park | Tip The Tyneside Irish Centre is on nearby St Andrew's Street, and
is a popular meeting place for the city's Irish community, while extending a welcome to all
(www.tynesideirishcentre.com).

18 City Baths, Newcastle

Rub-a-dub-tub

1838 was quite the year in north east England. During those momentous 12 months, the Newcastle and Carlisle Railway opened – the first line to run east to west across England. In September, Grace Darling and her father, William, rescued survivors from the wreck of the *Forfarshire* on Big Harcar off the coast of Northumberland. And the first Turkish baths in Newcastle opened on Northumberland Road, offering a far safer watery experience than the *Forfarshire*. The original building was the work of John Dobson (see ch. 33) and cost the then princely sum of £9,500.

The mid-19th century was a time when most homes did not have running water. Keeping clean was an arduous task, involving kettles and tin baths. The water was often shared by the family too, with the youngest at the back of the queue and bathing in the dirtiest water. In 1846 and 1847 the *Baths and Washhouses Acts* were passed. These required local councils to offer bathing facilities to the populace, leading to more Turkish baths being built across the country. Newcastle City Council took over the Northumberland Road baths in 1858 and, by 1906, they were the largest indoor baths in public ownership in the country.

The current City Baths – incorporating the City Pool – was opened in 1928 when the old building was pulled down and replaced, with the neighbouring City Hall built at the same time. Legend has it that Victoria Wood wrote her *Turkish bath* sketch after a visit to the baths, before performing at City Hall later that evening. The new baths were popular throughout the rest of the 20th century, with the building gaining a Grade II listing in 1992. Unfortunately, in 2012, a hard-up Newcastle City Council proposed mothballing the baths as a cost-cutting measure. A vigorous campaign to save the baths led to their sympathetic £7.5-million restoration, followed by a grand reopening in January 2020.

THE CITY BATHS.

Address Northumberland Road, Newcastle, NE1 8SG, +44 (0)191 261 7207,
www.city-baths.co.uk | Getting there Bus 1, 33, 33A, 38, 38A, Q3 QuayCity and various
others to John Dobson Street; Metro to Haymarket (Yellow or Green Line) | Hours
Mon–Fri 8am–10pm, Sat & Sun 8am–4pm | Tip Northumberland Street, Newcastle's
main shopping street, is just a few minutes' walk from City Baths. Pedestrianised now,
remarkably Northumberland Street was once the route of the A1 through Newcastle.

19___City Library

Worrk yer (library) ticket

Newcastle's City Library is the latest addition to the town's wide range of civic buildings. A thoroughly modern building of steel and glass, it replaced the Central Library, a 1960s concrete design that few mourned when it was pulled down in 2007. One highlight of the new library are the thoroughly comprehensive local studies and family history resources. If you want to research your Geordie roots, the City Library should be your first stop on that journey.

'Geordie' refers to one of two things. A Geordie is someone who comes from Newcastle or Tyneside, or the dialect spoken by someone from the region. 'That gadgie owwa there's from the Toon, like', is a Geordie sentence describing a man some distance away who is from Newcastle, and therefore a Geordie.

The word Geordie derives from George. But who was George? And why did the name attach itself to Tynesiders? There are a number of theories. One is that George is, or rather was, a very common name in the region. Another possibility is that it refers to George Stephenson, a railway engineer from Newcastle and inventor of a miners' safety lamp, once commonly used in northern pits. Or it may be because Geordies were loyal to the Kings George I and II during the Jacobite rebellions of 1715 and 1745.

The Geordie dialect, with its distinctive musical lilt, is largely Anglo-Saxon with a hint of Viking thrown in. This makes it an ancient dialect with roots back to the Dark Ages, mere centuries after the Romans upped sticks and left Britain. Take the word *hyem* for instance. Liable to result in blank incomprehension when used outside the north east, it means home and is pronounced much the same way as it was in Old English. On the other hand *Spelk*, meaning a splinter of wood, has its roots in the Old Norse word *spelkur*. Fortunately, getting a *spelk* in the City Library is unlikely, but you will feel right at *hyem* there.

Address Charles Avison Building, 33 New Bridge Street West, Newcastle, NE1 8AX, +44 (0)191 277 4100 | Getting there Bus 36 to John Dobson Street – Laing Art Gallery or bus 12, 39 or 40 to Monument New Bridge Street; Metro to Monument (Yellow or Green Line) | Hours Mon, Wed & Fri 10am–5pm, Tue & Thu 10am–7pm, Sat 10am–2pm | Tip Beamish Museum is a living open-air museum that tells the story of the north east from the 1830s through to the 1950s (Beamish, County Durham, DH9 0RG, +44 (0)191 370 4000, www.beamish.org.uk).

20 The Cluny

Live and kicking

Mike Mould had a dream. He wanted to take plays and performances out of theatres and into the community; to reach the young, the old and the disadvantaged by putting on shows in youth clubs, village halls and day centres. And so, in 1969, he founded the Bruvvers Community Theatre Company. Then, in 1983, the company lost its home on Shields Road and a new venue was needed. This Mike found in the form of The Cluny, a derelict bonded warehouse in the industrial heart of the Ouseburn Valley.

The Cluny was designed by John Dobson, an architect who worked closely with Richard Grainger (see ch. 33). Five storeys high and with huge floor space, it was an enormous task to renovate. Once Mike owned the property – with money borrowed from his brother Roy – he moved in with just the bare essentials: a camping stove, frying pan and a mattress. Mike then began the conversion of The Cluny into a 'Fun Palace', taking his inspiration from theatre director Joan Littlewood, at whose academy he'd studied. Others, perhaps less kindly, took to calling Mike's project the 'Looney Warehouse'.

The top floor of The Cluny became a rehearsal space for the Bruvvers, along with a store for costumes. Mike converted his bare essentials into a flat, in which his family still live. In 1999, Mike opened The Cluny Bar followed by The Round Theatre, hoping to use the profits to fund his community theatre work. Sadly, Mike died in April 2020, but by then the Ouseburn Valley was home to a thriving artistic community – all owing a debt to Mike's creative spirit and vision for the area.

The Cluny is now a bar, with performance space and café, and The Round, now renamed Cluny 2, is also used for live music and comedy performances. It has a reputation for introducing new local bands, who often go on to success. Whenever possible the bar uses local and independent breweries to supply its ales and lagers.

Address 36 Lime Street, Ouseburn, Newcastle, NE1 2PQ, +44 (0)191 230 4474, www.thecluny.com | **Getting there** Bus 12, 39 or 40 to New Bridge Street–Blackfriars, then a 7-minute walk; Metro to Manors (Yellow Line), then a 14-minute walk, paid parking at the Ouseburn Arches Car Park on Stepney Bank | **Hours** Mon–Thu noon–11pm, Fri & Sat noon–midnight, Sun noon–11.30pm | **Tip** 36 Lime Street – in the same building as The Cluny, and another of Mike's legacies – is home to more than 40 artists and designers. The artists' studios can usually be visited during open studio events, exhibitions and events, or by appointment (36 Lime Street, Ouseburn, Newcastle, NE1 2PQ, +44 (0)191 261 5666, www.36limestreet.co.uk).

21 Collingwood Monument

From Tyne to Trafalgar

Overlooking the mouth of the River Tyne, the Collingwood Monument celebrates the life of Vice Admiral Cuthbert Collingwood, second in command to Admiral Horatio Nelson during the Battle of Trafalgar. Collingwood was born in Newcastle in 1748 and attended the Royal Grammar School in the city. At the age of 12 he volunteered as a sailor on HMS *Shannon*, under the command of his cousin Captain Richard Brathwaite. Over the last decades of the 18th century, Collingwood rose through the ranks, taking command of his own ship as captain in 1781.

By 1805, Britain and her allies had been at war with France for 10 long years. Under the leadership of Napoleon Bonaparte, France was the dominant power on continental Europe. For Napoleon this was not enough. Enraged by a blockade of France by the British Royal Navy, Napoleon planned to combine his naval forces with Spain, take control of the English Channel and invade Britain.

That plan came to a grinding halt on 21 October, 1805 off the coast of southern Spain, close to Cape Trafalgar. On that day, the French and Spanish ships decisively clashed with the Royal Navy. Collingwood's ship, the *Royal Sovereign*, the fastest in the British fleet, was first to engage the enemy. On seeing the *Royal Sovereign* pull ahead Nelson cried, 'See how that noble fellow Collingwood carries his ship into action!' In a mere five hours, thanks to Nelson's astute tactics, the British were triumphant.

Nelson did not see the victory. Shot by a sniper during the mêlée of battle, he was dead. It was left to Collingwood to take charge of the British fleet and accept the surrender of the French forces. For his role at Trafalgar, Collingwood became 1st Baron Collingwood and was awarded a pension of £2,000 per year. His monument, paid for by public subscription, was completed 35 years after his death and features four cannons from the *Royal Sovereign*.

Address Tynemouth, NE30 4DD | Getting there Bus 306 to Tynemouth Village; Metro to Tynemouth (Yellow Line), then a 14-minute walk; free parking for two hours at Priors Haven Car Park, paid parking at Spanish Battery Car Park | Tip The Land of Green Ginger on Tynemouth's Front Street is a quirky independent collection of food, gift and clothes shops housed in a disused Congregational church.

22 __ Cross House

Tyneside's Flatiron building?

It's a complicated business building a city. Ideally, you'd start from scratch and plan carefully so that life is made easier for everyone. Unfortunately, most cities do not have that luxury. Instead they grow in a largely disorganised way, with later development often constrained by decisions made decades or even centuries before. This knotty problem faced the architects commissioned to squeeze a building into the narrow and roughly triangular space between the junction of Westgate Road and Fenkle Street. The result was Cross House, designed by Cackett and Burns Dick and completed in 1911.

Six storeys high, Cross House is a handsome, slender office block, clad in luminous Portland Stone. Behind the stone is a reinforced concrete skeleton, a revolutionary building method developed by François Hennebique and first used in 1879. Hennebique's system used concrete as a fireproof wrapping around wrought iron beams, creating a strong and extremely safe structure. Ironically, this was put to the test a mere eight years after Cross House was completed.

A disconcerting quirk of celluloid film is its tendency to spontaneously combust. Once burning, it is extremely hard to put out as it creates its own oxygen as it melts. One of the first residents of Cross House was the film distributor Famous Players-Lasky, who had a film storage vault in the building's basement. On 23 December, 1919 fire broke out in the vault, quickly spreading up the stairs and lift shaft, trapping people higher up the building who now had no means of escape. To add to their problems, the ladders used by the city's fire brigade were not long enough to reach the upper floors. Sadly 12 people lost their lives that day, some from making a last desperate leap from the roof. However, the fact that Cross House still stands is a testament to Hennebique's innovative construction techniques.

Address Westgate Road, Newcastle, NE1 4XX | **Getting there** Bus 10, 11, 38 or 38A to Central Station Westgate Road (Stand L); Metro to Central Station (Yellow or Green Line) | **Hours** Viewable from the outside only | **Tip** Newcastle Arts Centre on Westgate Road is home to a range of art-related businesses, including an art gallery, performance space and the popular Jazz Café (67 Westgate Road, NE1 1SG, www.newcastle-arts-centre.co.uk).

23 __ Crown Posada

Una pinta de cerveza bonny lad

Newcastle does not want for pubs to choose from. Arguably the most atmospheric is the Crown Posada, just a few minutes' walk from Newcastle's Quayside. The second oldest pub in Newcastle, built in 1880 to a design by W. L. Newcombe, who also worked on the city's Royal Victoria Infirmary, it still retains its original Victorian plan form and architectural features. A particular highlight are the two Pre-Raphaelite-style stained-glass windows, one featuring a woman carefully pouring a pint, the other showing an extravagantly bewhiskered Tudor gentleman about to drink it. Below the second window is a wonderful screened-off snug, ideal for a private bevvy with friends. To keep drinkers entertained, the pub's 1941 record player is used to play a continuous stream of old hits.

The fact that the owners have resisted the urge to modernise the pub – other than sympathetic renovation – has led to the awarding of a Grade II listing. Perhaps more importantly, however, is the Crown Posada's entry on CAMRA's Regional Inventory of Historic Pub Interiors, one of the few pubs in the north east to win this accolade.

The Crown Posada was originally just the Crown. Legend has it that Posada – a Spanish word meaning 'inn' or 'resting place' – was added when the pub was owned by a colourful sea captain. He had made his fortune in India, before marrying a Spanish señorita. However, the captain also cannily kept a mistress in Newcastle, who eventually helped him run the pub.

In 2015, the pub's Iberian connection was unexpectedly reinforced when four Spanish murals were discovered under wallpaper during a refurbishment project. The red and black murals show scenes of Spanish life, including Flamenco dancing and a traveller riding a donkey through a Spanish landscape. The murals have since been carefully covered over, ready to be rediscovered the next time the pub is redecorated.

Address 31 The Side, Newcastle, NE1 3JE, +44 (0)191 232 1269, www.sjf.co.uk/our-pubs/crown-posada | **Getting there** Bus Q1/Q3 Quaylink to Quayside Guildhall; Metro to Central Station (Yellow or Green Line), then a 7-minute walk along Westgate Road to the Side via St Nicholas Street | **Hours** Mon–Wed noon–11pm, Thu 11am–11pm, Fri 11am–midnight, Sat noon–midnight, Sun noon–10.30pm | **Tip** Big Mussel, just a few doors down from the Crown Posada, is a highly-regarded seafood restaurant serving authentic Belgian food and traditional beers (15 The Side, Newcastle, NE1 3JE, +44 (0)191 232 1057, www.bigmussel.co.uk).

24 The Customs House

Repurposed

The Customs House in South Shields is a theatre, restaurant, art gallery, cinema and community space all rolled into one. Facing the River Tyne, the Grade II-listed building has a handsome façade decorated in a Renaissance style. As the name suggests, the building wasn't always a theatre but was originally a shipping office and customs post.

South Shields owes its existence to its proximity to the mouth of the Tyne and the North Sea beyond. Shields is a derivation of Scheles or fishermen's huts in Anglo-Saxon, a name that stuck after the building of a fishing port in 1245 by the Prior and Convent of Durham. Unfortunately for South Shields – and North Shields across the Tyne – Newcastle didn't want rival ports on the river stealing trade away. It was very much in Newcastle's best interests that both settlements remained small and unimportant fishing villages. The first sign of trouble came in 1267 when a band of merchants – led by Nicholas Scott, mayor of Newcastle – attacked North Shields and set fire to buildings. Newcastle then tried legal intimidation, petitioning King Edward I to restrict the trade of the two villages. In 1279, the king found in favour of Newcastle, banning North and South Shields from holding fairs and markets, and selling bread and beer.

It wasn't until 1848 that both towns were recognised as ports requiring their own customs houses, separate from the one in Newcastle. The first customs house was established in this year, replaced by the current building in 1864. Ironically, after waiting so long for recognition, the port of South Shields only had one century of prosperity. By the 1960s the customs house was largely abandoned and slowly falling into dereliction. The Tyne and Wear Development Corporation funded the building's renovation. And so, in 1994, the Customs House opened its doors, and it has been going strong ever since.

Address The Customs House, Mill Dam, South Shields, NE33 1ES, +44 (0)191 454 1234, www.customshouse.co.uk | **Getting there** Bus 10, E1 or T503 to Ferry Street–Coronation Street; Metro to South Shields (Yellow Line), then a 13-minute walk; free car park when attending performances and events (vehicle must be registered at the box office on arrival) | **Hours** Daily 10am–8pm | **Tip** The Steamboat nearby is an award-winning real ale pub with a traditional feel and a dog-friendly policy.

25 Devonshire Building

Heralding a low carbon future

The need to live a greener and more sustainable lifestyle is a responsibility shared by everyone. This applies to institutions too, a thought that led Newcastle University to commission possibly the greenest place in the city. The Devonshire Building, completed in 2004, is the University's commitment to sustainability literally made concrete.

The Devonshire Building is home to the University's multidisciplinary Environmental and e-Science Research Centre, a description that does nothing to convey how innovative the structure is. Walk around the outside though, and the first thing to note is the series of long horizontal slats covering the curved south face of the building. These are shades that move intelligently to regulate the temperature of the interior of the building, helping to stop rooms overheating while still allowing natural light inside. Further cooling is achieved through the use of an 8,700-gallon geothermal water storage tank linked to a series of heat exchangers. This reduces the need for a conventional air-conditioning system, which would emit gases that contribute to the effects of global warming. The water mainly comes from a rainwater harvest system, which directs rain down from the roof.

Also on the roof, visible when you step back far enough, is a 1,980-square-foot array of photovoltaic panels. These provide a peak output of 25kW in the summer months, and help to lessen the need for National Grid electricity. Demand for power is reduced further by the use of movement sensors that turn lights on or off, depending on whether a room is occupied or not.

All of these and other measures helps the Devonshire Building use approximately 30 per cent less energy than other buildings of the period. All of this cleverness contributed to the achievement of an Excellent rating by BREEAM, a distinction that might leave other offices green with envy.

Address Devonshire Terrace, Newcastle University, Newcastle, NE1 7RX | Getting there Bus 10, 11, 47, X 47 and various others to Claremont Road-Museum | Hours Viewable from the outside only | Tip The Newcastle University campus is also home to the Hatton Gallery, a collection of over 3,000 artworks from the past 600 years. Notable artists represented include Francis Bacon, Wyndham Lewis and Palma Giovane (www.hattongallery.org.uk).

26 Dockwray Square

Childhood home of a comic genius

There is something painfully funny about the discordant jangle of a piano crashing to the ground. If you want proof, just watch Laurel and Hardy's 1932 short film *The Music Box*. If you are not curled up in a ball from laughter by the closing scene you either have no soul or you own a piano. Although the action largely takes place on steep steps in the Silver Lake district of Los Angeles, there is a direct link between *The Music Box* and North Shields.

Arthur Stanley Jefferson – better known as Stan Laurel – was born in 1890 in the town of Ulverston, then Lancashire now Cumbria. The Jeffersons were a family with the theatre in their blood. Stan's parents, Arthur and Margaret, were both actors, with Arthur senior also managing various theatres in northern England and Scotland. It was as the new manager of the Theatre Royal in North Shields, that Arthur senior moved his family to the town in 1897, to live at 8 Dockwray Square. It was a fine choice. Old photographs show neat terraced housing overlooking the River Tyne and the North Shields docks below. In the late 19th century, the docks would have been thick with fishing boats and an exciting place for an inquisitive young boy to explore.

The terrace is long gone, swept away during the 1950s in favour of flats that have in turn been replaced by modern housing. In 1989, Stan's North Shields childhood was commemorated by the erection of a sculpture at the centre of the square.

In 1901, the Jeffersons moved on to Bishop Auckland, to oversee another corner of Arthur senior's theatrical empire. And there the Tyneside connection with Stan Laurel's childhood appears to end. But does it? The steep steps down from Dockwray Square to the docks resemble those in *The Music Box*. Legend has it that these steps, and Stan's childhood memory of climbing them, were all the inspiration he needed to create 30 minutes of classic comedy.

Address Dockwray Square, North Shields, NE30 1JZ | Getting there Bus 333 to Bell
Street – Fish Quay; free parking at the Low Lights Car Park | Tip There is a good choice
of fish and chip shops, restaurants and pubs along Fish Quay.

27 __ Dog Leap Stairs
Brace for a ruff landing

If you want to keep fit in Newcastle you could do worse than to walk up and down Dog Leap Stairs a few times every day. This steep and narrow route is the most beloved of the city's quayside chares (see ch. 15). There are 80 steps in total that take you up from the broad, open space of the Side, to Castle Garth and the Black Gate. On one side of Dog Leap Stairs is the homely brick wall of one the Side's many office buildings; on the other are the vertiginous stone pillars of an intercity railway bridge, across which trains thunder from Newcastle Central Station *en route* to Scotland. Look into one of the arches of the bridge, about two-thirds of the way up, to see the remains of a stone wall. This is all that is left of a wall that once joined the Black Gate and City Keep but which was lost when the bridge was constructed.

Though slightly unprepossessing, Dog Leap Stairs have nevertheless been an inspiration to northern songwriters such as Kathryn Tickell, whose first album was named *Dog Leap Stairs*, and Mark Knopfler of Dire Straits, who name-checked the stairs in the song *Down to the Waterline* in 1978.

Dog Leap Stairs may have played their part in the drama of Bessie Surtees' elopement (see ch. 7). According to local legend, Bessie and her suitor, John Scott, rode a horse up the steps on the night that they fled to Scotland. How a horse, laden with two people, was persuaded to climb the steps is not recorded, nor whether the horse was given time to recover afterwards.

Another mystery is where the name Dog Leap comes from. Leap was recorded on pre-20th century maps as Loup and even Loop. Unfortunately, there is absolutely no evidence to suggest daring canine gymnastics ever took place here. The most likely reason is that Dog Leap Stairs gently curves at one point along its length, which from above – if you squint a bit – resembles the hind leg of a dog.

Address Side, Newcastle, NE1 3JE | **Getting there** Bus Q1/Q3 Quaylink to Quayside Guildhall; Metro to Central Station (Yellow or Green Line), then a 7-minute walk along Westgate Road to the Side via St Nicholas Street | **Tip** The cunningly named UpSide Down Presents sits at the foot of Dog Leap Stairs, and specialises in Newcastle-themed gifts for the discerning shopper, with coffee on the side.

28 Duke of Wellington

Pub landlord a towering success

Having a unique selling point is a useful attribute for any business, but particularly so if you're a publican in a city awash with pubs. The Duke of Wellington on High Bridge can claim to have once had a publican who *was* the USP.

William Campbell was a larger-than-life character. He was born in 1856 to a poor family living in a Glasgow slum. By the age of 10 he weighed 18 stone, and during his teenage years his weight was close to 40 stone. Not only that. At 6 foot 8 inches in height he towered over the rest of his family. Unfortunately, William's size and weight limited his opportunities in life. His dream was to train as a printer but he struggled to find employment. Eventually he ended up in a freak show, put on display in London wearing Highland dress and billed as the 'Scottish Giant'. By this time his weight had reached a staggering 52 stone, making walking difficult. Although freak shows are a horrendous concept to modern sensibilities, William doesn't seem to have been miserable with his lot in life. He even joked with the visitors who flocked to see him.

In 1877, with his wife Polly, William took on the lease of the Duke of Wellington. William was now not a well man. Although not a drinker, he smoked heavily and had a weak heart. Although Polly took on most of the work due to William's ill health, he was a major draw for the pub. Sadly however, he did not have long to enjoy his new role as publican. On 28 May, 1878, William died after a serious illness. On the day of his funeral his coffin was led through the city on a horse-drawn hearse. His death had been noted in local newspapers and so thousands filled the streets, eager to see the procession. He was buried in Jesmond Cemetery, the ceremony watched by thousands more. So, if you find yourself in the Duke of Wellington, raise a glass to William Campbell. He was a true giant of a man in every way.

Address 18 High Bridge, Newcastle, NE1 1EN, +44 (0)191 230 3002 | Getting there Bus 53 Voltra, X24, X24A or X34 to Pilgrim Street; Metro to Monument (Yellow or Green Line) | Hours Daily noon–10pm | Tip The Newcastle and District Branch of the Royal Scottish Country Dance Society runs regular events across the north east region throughout the year. All are welcome, with classes available for those who've not danced before or are just feeling rusty (www.rscds-newcastle.org).

29 Dunston Staiths

Europe's largest timber structure?

Coal was once the fuel that kept the British Isles snug and warm. The black rock also kept commerce humming along, powering both industry and the trains that moved goods around the country. Key suppliers of this carboniferous bounty were the collieries of Northumberland and County Durham.

London had a huge appetite for northern coal. The simplest way to move coal in quantity to the capital was by rail from the collieries to the River Tyne, and then by colliers down the eastern coast to the Thames. And so, in 1893, the Dunston Staiths were built. Owned by the North Eastern Railway Company, the staiths were essentially a harbour for the loading of coal onto the waiting colliers. At 1,726 feet long and 66 feet high, and built from pitch pine, the staiths are believed to be the largest timber structure in Europe. By the 1920s over 140,000 tons of coal passed along the staiths every week.

During their working life, the Staiths were operated by two groups of men: teemers and trimmers. Teemers were responsible for moving coal wagons along the staiths, as well as opening the wagon bottoms so that the coal could 'teem' down chutes into the holds of a collier below. Once the hold was filled, the trimmers would level the coal to make the collier stable and safe to sail. This was hard and dirty work, particularly during the dark winter months. For this reason, trimmers were better paid than the teemers. Despite this difference, both shared a room in the nearby Dunston Excelsior Club; anyone wandering into the room who didn't work on the staiths, or who wasn't there by invitation, was forcibly ejected.

The demand for coal declined in the final decades of the 20th century and so the staiths were abandoned and gradually fell into disrepair, suffering a serious fire in 2003. Since then, thanks to a Grade II listing, the staiths have been restored and opened to the public.

Address Staiths Road, Dunston, NE11 9DR, +44 (0)191 260 2133,
www.dunstonstaiths.org.uk | **Getting there** Bus 6, 10 Tyne Valley Ten, 45 X-lines and
various others to Team Street – Gas Works Bridge Road; free parking at the west end of the
staiths on Staiths Road | **Hours** Wed 10am – 7pm, Sat & Sun 10am – 5pm, bank holidays |
Tip The Staiths Café offers a varied and freshly made menu, as well as displaying work by
local artists (1 Autumn Drive, Staiths Southbank, NE8 2BZ, thestaithscafe.co.uk).

30 Elevated Walkway

One man's lofty ambitions made concrete

Hidden behind the Bridge Tavern, and under the Tyne Bridge, is an elevated walkway that ends abruptly a giddy 79 feet or so above the ground. Try to get onto the walkway and you find your way blocked by a forbidding metal gate.

To make sense of this you need to look at the life of T. Dan Smith, leader of Newcastle City Council between 1960 and 1965. Smith, along with chief planning officer Wilfred Burns, believed that Newcastle could become the 'Brasilia of the North'. This would be achieved by tearing down many of the city's tired 18th and 19th-century buildings and replacing them with Modernist architecture. Newcastle would become a multi-level city too, with a network of flyovers and pedestrian walkways weaving above, under and around buildings. It was a bold plan, but one that had a fatal flaw: T. Dan Smith.

Smith was a visionary and a supporter of both education and the arts. He also wanted to improve housing for the people of Tyneside. For these reasons, as well as for his enthusiastic advocacy of the city, he was nicknamed 'Mr Newcastle'. Unfortunately, he was also corrupt. Smith ran a public relations firm that specialised in the promotion of urban renewal across the country. Smith encouraged other councils to use the architect John Poulson for their own redevelopment schemes. He did this by adding councillors to his company's payroll in return for their support of Poulson in city planning meetings. For this, Smith allegedly received £156,000 from the architect. In 1973 Smith was arrested and accused of corruption. In 1974 he was put on trial, found guilty of the charges and sentenced to six years' imprisonment.

Ultimately Smith's vision for Newcastle never fully came to pass. His dream of a multi-level city sputtered out and was forgotten about. The elevated walkway that goes nowhere is a strangely apt metaphor for those times.

Address Akenside Hill, Newcastle, NE1 3UF | Getting there Bus Q1/Q3 Quaylink to Quayside Guildhall | Tip There has been a pub on the site of the Bridge Tavern for nearly two centuries. The current building is a replacement for one that was demolished in 1925 during the building of the Tyne Bridge. The Bridge Tavern has its own microbrewery, which is run in conjunction with Wylam Brewery.

31 The Fever Hospital
Out of fettle, pet?

The Fever Hospital, otherwise known as the House of Recovery, was built in 1804 at the cost of nearly £1,800, of which £1,438 2s. was raised by public subscription. (£1,800 is approximately equivalent to £80,000 now, so the hospital was a significant investment for the city.) Although close to the centre of modern Newcastle, when new the Fever Hospital was very much outside the boundaries of the city and built in an airy and undeveloped spot. And for good reason. The hospital was intended to house patients suffering from a variety of infectious ailments such as typhus, smallpox and cholera. These diseases were common in Newcastle at the time, particularly among working-class families. The hospital took in both poor and paying patients, with physicians from the dispensary looking after the patients. Records of the time show that overcrowding was a common problem in the hospital. Admission would have been a terrifying prospect, and many patients must have thought that they were unlikely to leave.

Cholera was perhaps the most feared. In one particularly vicious outbreak in September 1853, 1,527 people in Newcastle were killed by the disease. At the time, the cause of cholera was thought to be miasmas, or bad air from rotting vegetation and animal matter. It is now known that cholera is a gastrointestinal infection caused by the bacterium *Vibrio cholerae*, typically caught by drinking contaminated water. The 1853 outbreak occurred after water was pumped into the city's supplies from a tidal reach of the Tyne near Elswick.

The Fever Hospital closed in 1888 following the opening of the City Hospital for Infectious Diseases at Walkergate. For almost 100 years it was used by students of the Rutherford College, built nearby in 1878. In the 1980s the college was demolished to create the Bath Lane car park, leaving the Fever Hospital in fitting isolation once more.

Address Bath Lane, Newcastle, NE4 5SQ | **Getting there** Bus 71, 72 or 87 to Central Station Westgate Road, then a 5-minute walk; paid parking at The Gate Car Park | **Tip** Bath Lane is close to 'The Hill', a 437-yard stretch of Westgate Road dominated by independent motorbike showrooms and accessory stores. A visit is worthwhile even if just to watch bikers ride up and down the street, testing out their new machines.

32 Fiddler's Green Fisherman

When the boat comes in

Generations of fishermen have sailed from the quay at North Shields, off up the Tyne to the wild North Sea. Herring was their prize, to be sold on to markets in Newcastle and beyond. Fishing in the unpredictable waters off the British coast was, and still is, a dangerous business. Some of these men never returned, leaving broken families to mourn and weep and forever wonder at the fate of their missing husbands or fathers.

Perhaps a small crumb of comfort was the thought that their loved ones had reached Fiddler's Green, an afterlife for fishermen and sailors lost at sea. There the newly arrived lost soul, possibly soaked to the skin and distressed by his recent experience, would be greeted with a tot of rum and a pipeful of tobacco. Revived, he could then start to appreciate the happy prospect of eternal mirth and merriment with friends and comrades, accompanied by non-stop fiddle music and dancers who never tired.

Where and when the idea of Fiddler's Green originated is a mystery. One theory is that it was pirates who, less likely to get into a Christian heaven than most, invented their own paradise in which to while away eternity. It may even be a reinvention of the Elysian Fields, where Ancient Greeks who had lived a heroic or virtuous life would get their final reward.

Constructed from Corten steel, the Fiddler's Green Fisherman is a fitting tribute to the many North Shields fishermen lost at sea over the centuries. It was commissioned after extensive fundraising by the North Shields Fishermen's Heritage Project, and created by Seaham steel fabricator Ray Lonsdale. The two-ton sculpture is based on a photo of a local fisherman, taken by Harry Hann in the late 1950s. Just like the subject of the photo, the Fiddler's Green Fisherman looks thoughtfully out to the River Tyne – possibly thinking about long-lost friends and where they might be now.

Address North Shields, NE30 1JE | **Getting there** Bus 333 to Union Road–Fish Quay; free parking at the Low Lights Car Park | **Tip** The nearby Low Lights Tavern is the oldest pub in North Shields. A free house, the pub offers a wide range of guest ales and home-cooked food (Brewhouse Bank, North Shields, NE30 1LL).

33 Grainger Town
Classical ambition

Cities are never finished. Every generation of architects and city planners likes to tinker by replacing old buildings with new, or – for those with more ambition – through the extensive remodelling of whole districts. For centuries Newcastle has been prodded and poked, nipped and tucked in a variety of ways, though arguably never with as much graceful beauty as within the area known as Grainger Town.

Richard Grainger was born in 1797 into a poor family living in Low Friar Street. His father was a Quayside porter who died when Grainger was young. Educated in a charity school, Grainger set up a building business in 1816 with his brother George, who died just one year later. During his first decade as a builder, Grainger completed Eldon Square (see ch. 60), the success of which led to an appreciation of his talents by the great and the good in Newcastle.

In 1834, Grainger drew up ambitious plans for a large-scale redevelopment of Newcastle. With the backing of John Clayton – a wealthy town clerk and antiquarian – these plans were approved. To judge how ambitious Grainger's plans were, try to imagine Newcastle without these buildings: the Grainger Market, the Central Exchange or Theatre Royal. Grainger's plan added 32 inns and pubs, 325 shops and houses, and nine whole streets. Simply put, central Newcastle wouldn't have the classical character it has now without Grainger, or his architects Thomas Oliver and John Dobson.

The jewel of Grainger Town has to be Grey Street, the elegant beauty of which has been described as 'the finest street in Europe'. Perhaps the most effusive celebration was that of poet John Betjeman who wrote: 'I shall never forget seeing it to perfection, traffic-less on a misty Sunday morning. Not even Regent Street can compare with that subtle descending curve.' Who could argue with that? Other than people who live on Regent Street, possibly.

Address Newcastle, NE1 | Getting there Bus 1, 22, 22X, 53 Voltra, 71, 72, 87, 91N or Q2/Q3 Quaylink to Monument Market Street; Metro to Monument (Yellow or Green Line) | Tip The Bacchus is the third pub with this name in Newcastle. The current pub dates from the early 2000s and has a grand ocean liner theme to reflect Newcastle's shipbuilding heritage (42–48 High Bridge, Newcastle, NE1 6BX, +44 (0)191 261 1008).

34 Grey's Monument

Local lad does good

Standing at the centre of Newcastle, Grey's Monument commemorates the 19th-century Prime Minister Charles Grey, 2nd Earl Grey. Northumberland-born, Grey has two claims to historical fame. The first is as the Earl Grey of Earl Grey tea – a black tea flavoured with oil extracted from bergamot orange rind. Strangely, there is no agreement on why Grey's name is associated with the tea. One (likely apocryphal) story is that Grey preferred this blend over ordinary tea, as the perfumed flavour masked the taste of minerals in the water at his home in Howick.

Grey's Monument is not, however, a tribute to the Earl's taste in hot beverages, but to celebrate his important role as champion of the Great Reform Act of 1832. This Act of Parliament extended the voting franchise to include anyone who owned property worth £10 or more, and also abolished corrupt pocket boroughs. Although the act did not introduce a modern, representative democracy to Britain, it is now seen as an important step forward.

Grey's Monument was opened in 1838, with construction costs met by public subscription. It is a 130-foot Doric column, topped by a statue of Grey sculpted by the artist Edward Hodges Baily. The statue has looked south down Grey Street towards the River Tyne ever since, not counting the time that the head fell off after being struck by lightning in 1941. In 1947, a new head was created by Roger Hedley, reusing as much of the surviving original head as possible.

Inside the column are 164 steps that wind their way up to a viewing platform below Grey. At certain times of the year, the monument is open to a select number of pre-booked visitors who, after a strenuous climb, are rewarded with a wonderful – and unique – 360° view across the rooftops of the city. Even if you miss the opportunity, the area around the monument is a splendid place for people-watching every day of the week.

Address Blackett Street, Newcastle, NE1 7AL | Getting there Bus 12, 32, 32A, 62, 63, X63
to Newcastle Monument; Metro to Monument (Yellow or Green Line) | Hours Tours to
climb Grey's Monument are limited to 8 people per tour and only run on certain Saturdays,
Apr–July, 10am–4pm, and last 30 minutes. Tickets, booked through newcastlegateshead.com
are bought ahead of time and typically go on sale in February, though they quickly sell out. |
Tip Grey's Monument is next to the entrance of Grey's Quarter in intu Eldon Square, the
main food and drink area in the shopping centre.

35 High Bridge Quarter

Newcastle's hidden shopping gem

High Bridge Quarter includes High Bridge, one of the few cobbled streets in Newcastle, Upper High Bridge and Old George Yard. The area is a small, but characterful, shopping district. Perhaps the oddest aspect of High Bridge is the lack of a bridge. There once *was* a bridge, over the Lort Burn, which flowed down what are now Grey Street and Dean Street. The burn was covered over in 1784 as it was 'a vast nauseous hollow… a place of filth and dirt'. The superfluous bridge was pulled down, but the name stuck.

There are two historically-interesting pubs in High Bridge: the Duke of Wellington (see ch. 28) and the Old George Inn, the oldest pub in Newcastle. The latter is a 16th-century former coaching inn, said to be haunted by the ghost of King Charles I. In 1646, the king was held captive by the Scots in nearby Anderson Place during their occupation of Newcastle (see ch. 106). Although a prisoner, legend has it that Charles was occasionally allowed to visit the inn, presumably to sup a pint or two. In the Charles I Room is a chair in which the king is said to have sat. Visitors to the room have reported seeing the ghost of Charles – in the shapeless form of grey mist – sitting in this very chair.

A more contemporary thrill can be found in RPM, an independent record shop specialising in vinyl and CD. RPM can even sell you a carefully refurbished Hi-Fi or radiogram should you lack the wherewithal to play LPs. If you prefer your entertainment live rather than recorded, then pop into The Stand. Purpose-built, The Stand offers a varied programme of live comedy, with something for everyone's tastes. You can even give comedy a go by getting up on stage during The Stand's weekly beginners' night. And, if your routine goes down like a lead balloon, you could always go to the Old George Inn to drown your sorrows. Just be sure to steer clear of the spirits. And do not lose your head either…

Address High Bridge, Newcastle, NE1 6BX | **Getting there** Bus 53 Saltwell Park, X24, X24A or X34 to Pilgrim Street; Metro to Monument (Yellow or Green Line) | **Hours** Open all year round, though individual shops in the High Bridge Quarter have their own opening and closing times | **Tip** BALTIC 39 is an offshoot of BALTIC (see ch. 6), and is a community of practising contemporary artists (High Bridge, Newcastle, NE1 1EW, www.baltic.art/baltic-39).

36 High Level Bridge
Up above the River Tyne

Of the seven bridges that connect Newcastle and Gateshead, the High Level Bridge is strangely unregarded. Possibly this is because it doesn't have the visual flair of its near neighbours. It lacks the swooping suspension arches of the Tyne and Millennium Bridges, or the jaunty primary red colour scheme of the Swing Bridge. The High Level Bridge is… functional, a bit plain and frumpy. As a result it really doesn't get the love it deserves.

This is unfair on the High Level Bridge as it's a wonderful example of Victorian engineering. It even has a few unique points of its own, including the fact that it's both a road *and* rail bridge, trains rattling above traffic on their own deck. (At a giddy 120 feet above the River Tyne, there is no view finer of Newcastle and Gateshead than from a train crossing the bridge.)

Completed in 1849, the High Level Bridge was designed by Robert Stephenson, who was the son of railway pioneer George Stephenson. It was built to allow a rail connection from Scotland into the English network. During the bridge's construction, 130 families were moved and their homes demolished. The bridge is the height it is so that the rail deck is at the same level as the Brandling Junction Railway line in Gateshead.

The atmospheric pedestrian walkways over the High Level Bridge are a draw to filmmakers, though typically as a location in tense crime dramas rather than romantic comedies. In the iconic *Get Carter*, Jack Carter (Michael Caine) confronts Margaret (Dorothy White), his brother's mistress, midway across the bridge, before running to Newcastle to escape pursuers. In the slightly less iconic *Stormy Monday*, the bridge was again used for a confrontation, this time between characters played by Sting and Tommy Lee Jones. So, even if the High Level Bridge is overshadowed by its neighbours, it can rightfully make a claim to being a Hollywood superstar.

Address Newcastle, NE8 2BH | **Getting there** Bus Q1/Q3 Quaylink to Quayside Guildhall, then a 5-minute walk along Sandhill and up Castle Stairs (see ch. 15), or bus 27 Crusader, 56 Cityrider, 57 Citylink, 58 Citylink and various others to High Level Bridge North End; paid parking at Close/Swing Bridge Car Park | **Tip** The Bridge Hotel at the Newcastle end of the High Level Bridge is a traditional pub with great views of the River Tyne's bridges from its outdoor terrace (Castle Square, Newcastle, NE1 1RQ, +44 (0)191 232 6400, www.sjf.co.uk/our-pubs/bridge-hotel).

37 Hillgate Stones

Oops

Near to St Mary's Church in Gateshead is a jumble of large rocks. In the early morning of 6 October, 1854 these rocks were blasted into the air from Hillgate to rain down on the church. The Great Fire of Gateshead and Newcastle had begun.

Some time after midnight, flames were seen in the Worsted Manufactory of Messrs. Wilson and Sons on Hillgate. The fire quickly took hold and spread to a neighbouring building. Unfortunately, this was a warehouse in which huge quantities of nitrate of soda, brimstone, naphtha and manganese were stored. Excited spectators on the Newcastle quayside watched blue flames flickering in the night sky while firemen and soldiers of the 26th Regiment fought the blaze. And then – not long after 3am – came a massive explosion.

The force was so great that a six-foot beam of timber was later found on the roof of All Saint's Church. People in Seaham on the County Durham coast were said to have felt the shock from the blast. As hot metal and boiling sulphur fell onto other buildings, more fires started. Screams from the injured and the dying filled the air on both sides of the river. Some 53 people died that night, those close to the blast only identified by scraps of clothing or personal possessions.

The fire was so fierce that help was requested by telegraph. Fire crews from Hexham, Morpeth and Berwick came to assist. It took the whole of the day to extinguish the various fires. It was then that the devastation became apparent. A crater 40 feet deep and 50 feet wide was found where the warehouse had once stood. Newcastle's quayside was destroyed, with many buildings lost. The fact that St Mary's Church survived was thanks to the brave actions of a Mr James Mather, who entered the building with a hose and axe. The Hillgate stones are a poignant tribute to Mather and to all those who tackled the Great Fire on that dreadful night.

Address Hillgate, Gateshead, NE8 2AU | **Getting there** Bus Q1 Quaylink to Hillgate Quay; Metro to Gateshead (Yellow or Green Line), then an 8-minute walk; paid parking at Sage Gateshead Car Park and Church Street Car Park | **Tip** The neighbouring St Mary's Heritage Centre is the former parish church for Gateshead. The medieval building is now a visitor centre with displays showing the history of Gateshead, and family history records for the town.

38_Jarrow Hall
A little Anglo-Saxon learning

Long, long ago the north east was the centre of Christian learning in Britain. This was largely due to one man: The Venerable Bede. Bede was an Anglo-Saxon theologian and polymath who wrote books on a wide range of subjects, including astronomy, the nature of time, spelling, and natural history. He worked out that tides were caused by the influence of the moon; calculated the date that Easter should be celebrated; and taught that the world was round and not a flat disc. Bede's greatest achievement by far was his scholarly *Historia Ecclesiastica Gentis Anglorum*, or The Ecclesiastical History of the English People. Without this book the history of the Dark Ages would be darker still.

Bede was born in Monkton near Jarrow in ad 672 (or possibly 673). At the age of seven he was taken to a monastery in Wearmouth where he learned Greek and Latin. This sounds like cruel and unusual punishment for a likely blameless child, but it was the making of Bede. In ad 682, Bede moved to St Paul's Monastery in Jarrow. Remarkably, for someone who contemplated the deep mysteries of time and space, he never travelled further than York, spending almost his entire life in Jarrow. Bede died in May ad 735 and was canonised by Pope Leo XIII in 1899. He was first buried in Jarrow before his remains were moved to Durham Cathedral, where they've been ever since.

The place to go to find out more about Bede is the Jarrow Hall, Anglo-Saxon Farm, Village and Bede Museum. There you can wander round a delightful exhibition that guides you gently through Bede's life and legacy. Outside is a recreated Anglo-Saxon village, based on archaeological excavations in Northumberland. The draughty wattle-and-daub dwellings of the village convey a real sense of what life was like in 8th-century Britain. Enough to think that learning Latin and Greek in a snug monastery wouldn't be such a bad fate after all.

Address Church Bank, Jarrow, South Tyneside, NE32 3DY, +44 (0)191 424 1585,
www.jarrowhall.org.uk | Getting there Bus 27 Crusader or H1 to High Street; Metro
to Jarrow (Yellow Line), then an 18-minute walk; free parking at the museum | Hours
Thu–Sat 10am–4pm | Tip St Paul's Monastery in Jarrow is just 8-minutes' walk from
Jarrow Hall. The remains are largely medieval, but you can see parts of the original Anglo-
Saxon monastery, such as the chancel of St Paul's Church (www.english-heritage.org.uk).

39 __ Jesmond Dene

Armstrong's gift to the city

There could be only one winner if there were a prize for the most industrious Victorian Geordie, and that would be William George Armstrong. Starting his career as an attorney, Armstrong gave up law to pursue an interest in science and engineering. In 1840, at the age of 30, he invented a hydraulic engine, followed by a hydraulic crane that radically cut down the time it took to load and unload ships' cargoes on Newcastle's quayside. Over the next 60 years Armstrong's various engineering works supplied ships and armaments to both Britain and the world, with Armstrong amassing a vast fortune in the process.

With wealth came the opportunity to acquire land and property in Newcastle and Northumberland. One of Armstrong's many purchases was Jesmond Dene, a strip of woodland that follows the course of the Ouseburn Valley near Newcastle. In the 1850s, Armstrong enclosed his new possession and began to transform an untamed wilderness into landscaped parkland.

Armstrong had a lifetime fascination with water, and so one of the first improvements he made to the Ouseburn was the creation of a waterfall. To achieve the required drop, Armstrong had the underlying rock blasted out by explosive. A bridge was built directly in front of the waterfall so that visitors could stop and properly appreciate the scene. The Ouseburn was altered in other ways too, with large rocks added to affect the way the water flowed and to create a more dramatic landscape.

Initially, Jesmond Dene was a private space for Armstrong and his family, though twice a week it was opened to the public. The entrance fees collected on these days were donated to a local hospital. In 1883, Armstrong gifted Jesmond Dene to the Corporation of Newcastle upon Tyne. On 20 August, 1884, Jesmond Dene was officially opened by the Prince and Princess of Wales, since when it can be enjoyed all year round by everyone.

Address Jesmond, Newcastle, NE7 7BQ, www.jesmonddene.org.uk | **Getting there** Bus 6, 7, 8, 18, 18A, 38 and various others to Freeman Road – Hambledon Gardens; paid parking at Paddy Freeman's Car Park | **Tip** A popular food and drink market is held on Armstrong Bridge at the south end of Jesmond Dene every 1st and 3rd Saturday of the month (jesmondfoodmarket.co.uk).

40 John Woodger's Grave

Smoke me a kipper!

Some things are just so obvious and right that it's hard to believe that someone actually invented them. Take the kipper, for example, a herring that has been split, salted and then cured with smoke from a wood fire. Enter John Woodger, whose grave can be found in St John's Cemetery, Elswick.

Woodger was born in 1813. Originally from Hampshire, he moved to Newcastle at the age of 27 to take up the position of servant. However, not long after his arrival he was running a public house in Seahouses in Northumberland. In 1843, a shed belonging to Woodger – filled with salted herring – accidentally caught fire. The smoke cured the herring, creating the world's first kippers. Cannily, Woodger realised he had a tasty new product to sell. He made the most of his serendipitous discovery, establishing his first curing yard with his two brothers in North Shields, followed by a shop on Northumberland Street.

It's not an overstatement to say that the Victorians loved kippers, with the fish quickly becoming a cheap and nutritious mainstay of the British breakfast experience. The demand for kippers made Woodger a successful man, enabling him to acquire property all along the east coast. In 1858, he opened a curing yard in Great Yarmouth to take advantage of Norfolk's longer herring season. In 1889, kippers were given the ultimate accolade of being added to the breakfast menu of the Savoy Hotel, where they've remained ever since.

Unfortunately, there's just one tiny but inconvenient flaw in the story of Woodger's unplanned invention: it isn't true. While it can't be denied that Woodger did well out of kippers, the incident with his shed probably never happened. In fact, historians believe that people have been curing salted herring for centuries, probably for millennia. Despite this, the legend of Woodger and his smoke-filled shed persists – even if now it all seems a bit fishy.

Address St John's Cemetery, Elswick Road, Newcastle, NE4 8DL | **Getting there** Bus 30, 31 or 84 to Elswick Road–Eastgate Gardens or Elswick Road–St John's Cemetery; on-street parking nearby | **Tip** L. Robson and Sons have been smoking salmon and herring for almost a century. Their world-famous Craster kippers can be eaten at their restaurant in the village of Craster, or ordered online for home delivery (Haven Hill, Craster, Northumberland, NE66 3TR, www.kipper.co.uk).

41 Kenton Bunker

Tally ho!

The summer of 1940 was a desperate time for Britain. Across the English Channel and North Sea was a ruthless and well-armed enemy intent on invasion. Only the pilots of the RAF's Fighter Command stood in its way, ready to defend their country during what became known as the Battle of Britain. Although Kent and the south coast was the prime focus of Nazi attention, the industrial north was also a target. The aerial defence of northern England was the responsibility of Fighter Command's 13 Group, under the command of Air Vice-Marshal Richard Saul. Spitfires and Hurricanes, flying out from RAF Acklington in Northumberland and RAF Usworth in County Durham, tackled Luftwaffe bombers during raids in August.

Invasion was, of course, averted. War in Europe ground on for five more years but peace eventually came. After VE Day the north's RAF stations, once so important, were surplus to requirements. One by one they were closed: a prison was built at Acklington, and Usworth served briefly as Sunderland Airport but has now largely been subsumed by Nissan.

There is, though, one surviving site from that fateful summer. Kenton Bunker was 13 Group HQ, and an RAF Operations Room during the Battle of Britain. From there, Fighter Command's planes could be directed towards the enemy quickly and efficiently. In 1948, with a colder war looming, the bunker became a Regional War Room from where Civil Defence operations would be run after an atomic attack. However, even this role was temporary. By 2003 the site was a bureaucratic odd-sock drawer used by various government departments, from the Inland Revenue to the Driving Standards Authority.

Now the bunker stands empty, unused but not unloved. Surrounded by a new housing estate, its upkeep is in the hands of Secret Bunker North who, despite the name, want more people to know about this small but significant witness to history.

Address Ashover Road, Kenton, NE3 3GH, secretbunkernorth.org | Getting there
Bus 7, 8, 32, 32A, 111, 118, S 135 or T 1 to Kenton Lane – Hazeldene Avenue; free parking
at Cragston Car Park, then a 12-minute walk (parking for residents only at the bunker) |
Hours Viewable from the outside only | Tip North East Land, Sea and Air Museum
(NELSAM) at the former RAF Usworth site has a wide range of British military aircraft on
display, including the iconic Avro Vulcan (Old Washington Road, Sunderland, SR5 3HZ,
+44 (0)191 519 0662, www.nelsam.org.uk).

42 Kittiwakes

Feathered tourists fly in for summer

Newcastle and Gateshead receive their fair share of tourists from far and wide. However, none of these visitors returns as regularly as kittiwakes, a small species of gull. Each spring, at the start of the breeding season, kittiwakes fly into the city centre, colonising ledges, roofs and chimneys on buildings close to the Tyne. They are the UK's only urban colony of kittiwakes, and nest further inland than any other colony in the world.

Kittiwakes usually nest on the narrow ledges of sea cliffs and can also be found further north, on the craggy faces of Northumberland's Farne Islands. Why they have chosen to populate Newcastle is a mystery. The kittiwakes have only been nesting in the city since the 1960s, long after many of the buildings along the river were completed. Where they come from is less mysterious. They spend the winter months out at sea, often as far away as Canada, making them well-travelled visitors.

Approximately 600 pairs breed in the city. Each pair builds a nest made from plant material and mud. Each nest has a bowl-shaped indentation into which eggs are laid. Typically, two or three chicks are raised by a pair during the breeding season. Kittiwakes feed on fish, caught out at sea along the region's coastline. On return to the nest, the kittiwakes regurgitate the fish to feed their chicks.

Although the nests are well above head-height, there are many places to get close to the birds. The two best places, where you can get an almost eye-level view, are the viewing platform of the BALTIC and from the path across the Tyne Bridge. Kittiwakes are entertaining to watch. Kittiwake pairs bond by bowing their heads and putting on a food-begging display. It must work, as pairs are known to stay together for two years or more. You do not have long to see them though. By late summer the kittiwakes depart and the river is suddenly a much quieter place.

Address Tyne Bridge, Newcastle, NE1 3AE | Getting there Bus Q2/Q3 Quaylink to Quayside Guildhall | Tip The Farne Islands are host to a wide variety of seabirds, including puffins, Arctic terns and guillemots. During the summer season, boat trips regularly sail from the nearby port of Seahouses.

43 Lady Venus

Never clothed

Young Geordies take a certain masochistic pride in wearing the minimum amount of clothing when out for a good time in town. Even in the depths of winter you'll see them on the streets in tee-shirts and tops, coats being something only soft southerners wear. There are two ladies in Newcastle who go one better, however. They have spent over 85 years outdoors completely naked, the wind able to whistle unimpeded around their nether regions.

The Lady Venus figures stand on a pair of ornate clocks, one on the Northern Goldsmiths building on Blackett Street, the other on a building at the junction of Clayton Street and Westgate Road. Commissioned by Northern Goldsmiths in 1932 and designed by Alfred Glover, the Lady Venuses are both roughly life-sized and hold their arms aloft to symbolise progress.

As befits their status representing a goldsmith, they are covered in a fine layer of 24 carat gold leaf. The clock and Lady Venus on Blackett Street have recently been renovated, with the clock's quarterly chime reinstated after a long period of silence. During World War II the Blackett Street clock became a regular meeting place for servicemen and their girlfriends or wives. Earning the name of the 'kissing clock', numerous marriage proposals are known to have been made underneath since.

Northern Goldsmiths opened its first shop in Newcastle in 1778 on the Blackett Street site. This shop was replaced in 1892 by the current building, a wonderfully detailed structure designed by the architect James Cackett. The firm was the first UK stockist of Rolex, whose logo is emblazoned on the faces of the Lady Venus clocks. Northern Goldsmiths also made the marine chronometers used by Shackleton during his Antarctic expedition of 1921–22. Whether there were any Geordies on the expedition, and whether they declined to wear warm clothing when out on the ice, is sadly unrecorded.

Address Northern Goldsmiths, 1 Blackett Street, Newcastle, NE1 5AU, +44 (0)191 232 2264, www.goldsmiths.co.uk | Getting there Bus 30 or 31 to Monument Pilgrim street; Metro to Monument (Yellow or Green Line) | Tip The Hancock Gallery is a fine art gallery that shows the work of contemporary artists (2 Jesmond Road West, Newcastle, NE2 4PQ, +44 (0)191 241 0442, hancockgallery.co.uk).

44 Laing Art Gallery
Cheers!

Every city needs an art gallery. Newcastle has the splendid Laing Art Gallery, home to a varied collection of paintings and drawings. Wandering around the galleries you can view work by local artists, such as the apocalyptic visionary, John Martin, as well as delicate watercolours by the likes of Joseph Turner and Edward Lear. In the Northern Spirit room, the Laing also has a fine collection of local artefacts that tell the story of Newcastle and the north east.

The existence of the Laing is due to the generosity of Alexander Laing. At the start of the 20th century Newcastle did not have an art gallery. In 1900 in a letter to the Newcastle Corporation, Laing offered to fund the construction of a gallery. Laing was originally from Forfarshire, but moved to Newcastle in 1849 as a representative of Edinburgh brewers Jeffrey and Co. He then set up a bottling company in the town, before diversifying further as a wine merchant and hotel owner. The gallery opened in October 1904, just one year before Laing died at the age of 77.

Laing was not a collector of art so did not contribute artwork to the new gallery. The gallery's first curator, C. Bernard Stevenson, playfully suggested that wood shavings left by the building's joiners should be put on permanent display after the inaugural exhibition had closed. Laing did believe, however, in the generosity of the inhabitants of his adopted home town. His confidence that the gallery 'would soon be supplied with pictures and statuary for the encouragement and development of British Art', quickly proved right. Coincidentally, one early donor had also made his fortune through alcohol. A. H. Higginbottom was a wine and spirit merchant with a passion for Japanese art, who donated his collection to the gallery. Fortunately, those wood shavings were never needed, for generous donors have added to the Laing's collection ever since. And it is a collection that Newcastle can be rightly proud of.

In a word, what I wanted to do was create a style for our age.

Emile Bernard

Address New Bridge Street, Newcastle, NE1 8AG, +44 (0)191 278 1611, www.laingartgallery.org.uk | Getting there Bus 36 to John Dobson Street – Laing Art Gallery or bus 12, 39 or 40 to Monument New Bridge Street; Metro to Monument (Yellow or Green Line) | Hours Mon–Sat 10am–4.30pm | Tip The Biscuit Factory is an independent commercial art gallery housed in a former Victorian manufacturing building (16 Stoddart Street, Newcastle, NE2 1AN, +44 (0)191 261 1103, www.thebiscuitfactory.com).

45__Leazes Park
Newcastle's oldest park

With 33 in total, one thing that Newcastle does not lack is public parks. The oldest planned park in the city is Leazes Park, a leafy space sandwiched between the Royal Victoria Infirmary and St James' Park.

The land that is now Leazes Park was originally granted to the Freemen of Newcastle by King John for the grazing of cattle. In 1857, a petition signed by nearly 3,000 working men was handed in to Newcastle City Council. The successful petition demanded that an area of land be given over to create a free and open place of recreation for the people of the city. The area chosen was named Leazes Park – leazes means meadowland, or a place to gather crops – though for a while it was also affectionately known as the people's park.

The task of designing the park was initially given to John Hancock, the naturalist later instrumental in founding what is now the Great North Museum. Unfortunately, Hancock's ideas were rejected for being too grand and expensive, as well as lacking in areas for playing sport and games. Next, John Laing, after whom the Laing Art Gallery is named, was approached to propose a park design. Laing's more modest ideas were also turned down. The park that opened on 23 December, 1873 was an amalgam of the two men's plans, with a bit of tinkering here and there by a Mr Fulton, who was Town Surveyor at the time.

In 1875, an ornate 10-sided bandstand was built in the centre of the park, and was used every Sunday to provide free musical entertainment. At some point in the 1960s the bandstand was pulled down, but a faithful replacement was built in 2003 – the design recreated from historical records. Since then an ongoing series of improvements has seen an extensive programme of tree planting, as well as the restoration of the boating lake. These improvements and additions make Leazes Park truly a park of and for the people.

So, take a stroll there as soon as possible.

Address Richardson Road, Newcastle, NE2 4BJ | **Getting there** Bus 32, 32A, 36 or 84A to RVI–Dental Hospital; free 2-hour parking at Leazes Park Car Park, paid parking at Leazes Park Road Car Park | **Tip** *The Flowering of the Lort Burn* artwork that cuts across Leazes Park follows the route of an underground stream that provides the water for the boating lake, and continues on under Grey Street to the Tyne.

46 Lit & Phil

Intellectual discourse

The Literary and Philosophical Society of Newcastle upon Tyne – or Lit & Phil – is the UK's largest subscription library outside London. Founded in 1793 as a 'conversation club', members would meet to discuss science, literature and other intellectual issues of the day. Initially the members met in a variety of different buildings in Newcastle. However, donations of books and curiosities soon led to the need for a more permanent residence. This resulted in the construction of a handsome Georgian building on Westgate Road. Completed in 1825, the Lit & Phil still calls this home today.

After more than two centuries of acquisition, the Lit & Phil now has over 170,000 books in its library with the collection growing by 1,000 books every year. Local history is particularly well represented, as are natural history, science and crime fiction (even intellectuals need to relax). As well as books, there are hundreds of classical music scores and over 10,000 LPs. A lifetime really isn't long enough to take advantage of the Lit & Phil.

One of the oddest curiosities received by the Lit & Phil were the shrunken remains of a newly wed couple from the Northumbrian town of Hexham. In 1800, two even stranger specimens arrived from Australia. A gift from Governor John Hunter of New South Wales, who was an honorary member of the society, the specimens were preserved in a cask of spirits. The first was a duck-billed platypus. The oddly hybrid nature of the creature must have fascinated the society members. The second specimen was called a 'wombach', which we now know as the wombat. In 1826, the skin was given to a taxidermist for stuffing and mounting. Unfortunately, the taxidermist had never seen a wombat in real life and so he mounted it in a standing position, similar to a kangaroo. It can still be seen in this unnatural posture in the Great North Museum today.

Hooray then for the Lit & Phil. A real talking point in the city.

Address 23 Westgate Road, Newcastle, NE1 1SE, +44 (0)191 232 0192, www.litandphil.org.uk |
Getting there Bus 10, 11 or 38 to Central Station Neville Street (Stand A), or bus 1, 30
or 31 to Central Station Neville Street (Stand B); Metro to Central Station (Yellow or Green
Line) | Hours Mon, Tue, Thu & Fri 10am–noon, 1–4pm; Wed 10am–noon, 1–4pm |
Tip The nearby Split Chimp is an independent micro pub serving real ales and ciders,
as well as bottled craft beers, and wines (Arch 7, Westgate Road, Newcastle, NE1 1SA,
www.splitchimp.pub).

47 _ Little Theatre

Taking centre stage in Gateshead

Some amateur theatrical groups perform wherever they can find a space, whether that be a draughty church hall or a modern community centre. The Progressive Players of Gateshead proudly do things differently.

The Progressive Players were originally the Gateshead ILP Dramatic Club, which was formed in 1920 and initially affiliated to the Independent Labour Party. The first plays by the company were put on in Westfield Hall on Alexandra Road. One of these early productions was George Bernard Shaw's *Pygmalion*. At a meeting of the British Drama League, attended by Shaw, a member of the Club caused much laughter by standing up to announce that she had seven shillings and fourpence in royalties for him.

Relations with the managers of Westfield Hall were strained during the 1930s, and so finding a new and more permanent home became necessary. In the summer of 1939, thanks to the generosity of three of the founder members, the Progressive Players were able to purchase 3 Saltwell View and a neighbouring empty lot, where a new theatre could be built.

This was unfortunate timing. Due to the outbreak of war, work on the theatre halted. For two years, 3 Saltwell View was used as a barrage balloon station, until the building was handed back in 1941. Even during the privations of war, the Little Theatre began slowly to take shape. By the autumn of 1943, enough of the theatre was complete that the company was able to perform *A Midsummer Night's Dream* to a paying audience. It is thought that the Little Theatre was the only new theatre built in Britain during World War II. In the decades since, the Progressive Players have continued to perform in the Little Theatre, usually to a full house. A varied programme and continuous development, including the purchase of 4 Saltwell View to provide rehearsal space and costume storage, has made the Little Theatre a big part of Gateshead life.

Address 1–4 Saltwell View, Gateshead, NE8 4JS, +44 (0)191 478 1499, www.littletheatregateshead.co.uk | **Getting there** Bus 54 Voltra to Saltwell Park; parking on Saltwell View and neighbouring streets | **Tip** Saltwell Park, the main entrance to which is opposite the Little Theatre, is a large green space with facilities such as tennis and basketball courts, and dog-walking areas.

48 Low and High Lights

Bringing seafarers safely home

GPS has made navigation a whole lot easier than it once was. It's not that long ago in the scheme of things that getting to your destination required maps, compass, and a lot of skill with a good dollop of luck. Navigating on sea added the extra hazard of grounding in shallow water, or even wrecking on rocks. Entering port was often no better. Rivers can be treacherous places too, which is why river pilots – with their knowledge of safe routes along rivers – are still used to steer ships into harbour today.

The Low and High Lights of North Shields were leading lights – a visual safety aid for ships and boats entering the River Tyne. There are two sets of lights, the Old High and Low Lights, and the High and Low Lights. The Old lights – unsurprisingly – came first and were commissioned in the 1530s, though the original buildings were replaced by the current structures in 1727. Initially, three tallow candles were used to provide light, before their replacement by oil lamps in 1773. By aligning the two lights – one above the other – sailors could steer their boats along a safe channel into harbour.

By 1805 – due to the ever-changing nature of the river bed – the two lights no longer aligned with a safe route into the Tyne. The lights were decommissioned, with the Old High Light painted black to avoid confusion with its replacement. Both old lights were then converted to almshouses in 1830.

The new Low and High Lights were completed in 1810, with the lights lit for the first time on 1 May that year. As technology improved, the lights were upgraded: first to gas in 1861, and then to electricity in 1927. Ironically, the wrecking of the *Friendship* and the *Stanley* in 1864 (see ch. 104) occurred because the lights weren't operational that day. Despite this blot, the new lights provided an invaluable service all the way up to their decommissioning in the late 1990s.

Address Clifford's Fort, North Shields Fish Quay, NE30 1JA | Getting there Bus 333 to
Union Road – Fish Quay then a 6-minute walk; free parking at the Low Lights Car Park |
Tip The Old Low Light Heritage Centre tells the story of North Shields maritime history.
Open seven days a week, there is a rolling programme of exhibitions, a viewing platform,
shop and café (Clifford's Fort, North Shields Fish Quay, NE30 1JA, +44 (0)191 257 4506,
www.oldlowlight.co.uk).

49 Lying-in Hospital

Broadcasting to the region

You could easily walk past the slightly dowdy Lying-in Hospital. Built in 1826, the odd name refers to its original use as a maternity hospital for poor women to take bed rest before giving birth. It continued in this role until 1923 when the city's Princess Mary Maternity Hospital was opened.

In 1922, the British Broadcasting Company, as the BBC then was, made its first radio transmission from Newcastle. The BBC then took over the Lying-in Hospital in 1925, renaming it Broadcasting House. Until the late 1980s, local radio, and then television, was broadcast to the region from there. During the 1950s, radio programmes such as *Watcheor Geordie*, featuring well-known northern comedians like Bobby Thompson, were incredibly popular.

The flagship TV programme produced by BBC North East is the daily news show *Look North*. First broadcast in March 1968, *Look North* was originally hosted by Mike Neville, a role he held for 28 years. The avuncular Neville won many awards during his time on *Look North*, including an MBE for services to broadcasting. Neville also had the dubious honour of being pranked by Noel Edmonds on *Noel's Saturday Roadshow*, the only regional BBC anchor to receive the show's 'Gotcha' trophy. Today *Look North* is presented by Carol Malia, but no longer from the Lying-in Hospital.

Television technology constantly evolves. In 1988, the BBC left Newcastle city centre and moved into a new custom-built studio complex in Spital Tongues. Known locally as the 'Pink Palace' after its colour, the new Broadcasting House is a state-of-the-art facility used for both radio and television productions. *Look North* was first broadcast from its new home on 18 January, 1988, just a few months shy of its 20th anniversary. As for the Lying-in Hospital, it's now office space. Not an exciting fate given its history, but after babies and bulletins it's a more gentle existence.

Address New Bridge Street, Newcastle, NE1 8AL | Getting there Bus 12, 39 or 40 to
Monument New Bridge Street; Metro to Monument (Yellow or Green Line) | Hours
Viewable from the outside only | Tip Trillians Rock Bar has been the go-to venue for rock
and heavy metal fans since the 1980s. Regular live shows entertain drinkers throughout the
year (Princess Square, Newcastle, NE1 8ER, +44 (0)7710 095 238, trilliansnewcastle.co.uk).

50 Maddison Memorial

Family matters

The Cathedral Church of St Nicholas, or Newcastle Cathedral, is one of the city's must-see places. The main body of the church dates from the 14th century and is in the Perpendicular style. Crowning the tower is a lantern spire, which was used as a navigation aid for ships sailing up the Tyne. Inside are many delightful details, including a memorial to Lord Collingwood (see ch. 21), who was married in the cathedral in 1791. However, perhaps the most touching monument in the cathedral is the Maddison Memorial, found in the south aisle.

Henry Maddison and Elizabeth Barker were married in the cathedral in 1594. Henry was a coal-mining industrialist and later Mayor of Newcastle. During the course of their marriage Henry and Elizabeth had 16 children, 15 of whom survived into adulthood. The memorial was commissioned by the couple's eldest son, Lionel, soon after the death of his father in 1634. Following the family tradition, Lionel also became Mayor of Newcastle. In 1633, during his mayoral year, Lionel was knighted by King Charles I, who was on his way north to be crowned in Scotland.

As befits such a distinguished family, the memorial is splendidly elaborate. Sculpted in marble, it has been carefully and colourfully painted. Each member of the family is represented by a beautifully carved figure. Henry and Elizabeth, kneeling in prayer, naturally take centre stage. Sir Lionel, Henry's father, with his wife, Jane Seymour, kneel to Henry's left. To Elizabeth's right is Lionel himself, with his wife Anne Hall behind. Below are the small but detailed figures of Henry and Elizabeth's children; ten brothers on the left and six sisters on the right. One of the sisters is a toddler. This is Susan, who died not long after her first birthday in 1603. Her inclusion, many years after her death, is a moving indication of how important the Maddisons were to each other.

Address Newcastle Cathedral, St. Nicholas Square, Newcastle, NE1 1PF, newcastlecathedral.org.uk | **Getting there** Bus 27 Crusader, 56 Cityrider, 57 Citylink, 58 Citylink and various others to High Level Bridge North End | **Hours** Mon–Fri 7.30am–6pm, Sat 8am–4pm, Sun 7.30am–6pm | **Tip** Newcastle Cathedral is Anglican. The Cathedral Church of St Mary's is the city's Catholic cathedral and was designed by Augustus Pugin, famed for his design of the interior of the Houses of Parliament (Clayton Street West, Newcastle, NE1 5HH, www.stmaryscathedral.org.uk).

51 Mark Toney

Geordie gelato

Some years *really* are worth celebrating. 1892 is definitely one that Novocastrian ice cream lovers should commemorate. It was in this year that Giovanni Marcantonio – with wife Angela and baby son Antonio – left Picinisco in Italy determined to make a new life abroad. Marcantonio wasn't alone, for many Italians made similar journeys around this time. For many Italians, Britain was merely a stopping point on the longer journey to the United States. Giovanni however, went no further than Newcastle, later claiming – possibly tongue in cheek – that that was as far as his ticket would take him.

Once settled in Newcastle, Marcantonio began making ice cream, selling it on the streets from a hand cart. Made by combining cream, milk, eggs and sugar, Marcantonio's ice cream quickly proved popular. The ice cream was initially sold in penny lick glasses. A customer would pay a penny and receive a scoop of ice cream in the glass. The happy recipient would lick the ice cream out and return the glass, which would then be wiped clean for the next person. Unsurprisingly, penny licks were banned in 1926 for hygiene reasons. By this point Mark Toney was selling ice cream in wafers, a far safer and tastier way to enjoy ice cream!

Note the name change. After Giovanni retired, Antonio took over the business, anglicising Marcantonio and opening a permanent ice cream parlour in the Grainger Market, followed by one on Percy Street in the 1930s. Then, in 1962, the café on Grainger Street was opened. This is the flagship of the three Mark Toney parlours, and one that became the in-place for teenagers looking for love and romance during the swinging 1960s. Many of them in later life probably brought children and then grandchildren to Mark Toney. Today, Mark Toney is run by Anthony Marcantonio, Giovanni's great-grandson, who was born above the family's old ice cream factory in Byker.

Address 53 Grainger Street, NE1 5JE, +44 (0)191 232 7794, 91 Percy Street, NE1 7RW, +44 (0)191 232 1021, 30−31 Grainger Arcade, NE1 5QF, +44 (0)191 261 4403, www.marktoney.co.uk | Getting there Bus 1, 30 or 31 to Grainger Street; Metro to Central Station (Yellow or Green Line) for Grainger Street/Arcade parlours, or bus Q3 Quaylink, 46 X7 Max, X8 Max, X9 Max and various others to Haymarket Bus Station; Metro to Haymarket (Yellow or Green Line) for Percy Street parlour | Hours Mon−Sat 7.30am−8pm, Sun 9.30am−8pm | Tip Mark Toney is a near neighbour of Forbidden Planet, Newcastle's largest cult entertainment store, selling everything an SF or comic enthusiast could want in their life (49 Grainger Street, Newcastle, NE1 5JE, www.forbiddenplanet.com).

52 Marsden Bay

South Shields sea stacks by the sea shore

The long curve of Marsden Bay is one of the north east's geological wonders. The beach is bounded by cliffs of Magnesian Limestone, formed almost 250 million years ago during the Permian period. The sedimentary rock formed in a shallow tropical sea, at a time when Britain lay just north of the Equator and was part of the supercontinent of Pangea.

To reach the beach you first have to walk down a steep series of steps next to the Marsden Grotto (though the steepness is only really noticeable on the climb back up...). The Grotto was created in the 18th century by a miner named Jack 'the Blaster' Bates, who used explosives to create a cave at the base of the cliff face. This provided a rent-free beach-front property for Jack and his wife Jessie, as well as a place to store contraband for local smugglers. The Grotto has been an inn since the 19th century, with its patrons able to take a less physically-demanding lift down to the beach. The inn is allegedly haunted by the ghost of 'Jack the Jibber', who is believed to have been murdered by fellow smugglers after he sold them out to HM Customs. Until the tradition stopped in 1999, landlords would leave a tankard full of beer out overnight for Jack, which would be empty by the morning.

The most striking feature of Marsden Bay are its sea stacks. The largest of these is Marsden Rock, a substantial 98 feet high. Once part of the mainland, Marsden Rock is gradually shrinking due to tidal erosion. A rock fall created an arch in 1911, which lasted until the winter of 1996, when it too came crashing down. In the 19th century people paid for the privilege of climbing ladders to the top of the rock to eat picnics on its grassy top. The ladders and the grass are long gone. In the summer breeding season the rock is the exclusive home to colonies of fulmars, cormorants and kittiwakes, now undisturbed by the presence of people.

Address Coast Road, South Shields, NE34 7BS | **Getting there** Bus E1 to Coast Road – Marsden Grotto; paid parking at Marsden Beach Car Park | **Tip** Souter Lighthouse, just three-quarters of a mile away, is open to the public. A National Trust property, the lighthouse was the first in the world to be designed specifically to use electricity to illuminate its lamp. Highlights include an engine room and restored keeper's living quarters (www.nationaltrust.org.uk).

53 Martin Luther King Jr
A tribute to an American hero

There are some concepts that really don't belong together, like fish-fingers and custard. At first glance, Tyneside and Dr Martin Luther King Jr, Christian minister and American civil rights activist, don't seem to fit either. However, there is a connection, one celebrated by a bronze statue of King standing in Armstrong Quad, Newcastle University.

Martin Luther King Jr first came to prominence in 1955, leading a boycott of the segregated public transit system of Montgomery, Alabama. This came after the arrest of Rosa Parks for refusing to give up her bus seat to a white passenger. The boycott, after a ruling by the American Supreme Court, eventually led to the desegregation of Alabama's public transport. After this, King campaigned for black equality nationally, using non-violent civil disobedience – inspired by the techniques of Mahatma Gandhi. In 1964, King was awarded the Nobel Peace Prize for tackling racial inequality using non-violent methods.

King's life was a hectic whirl of campaigning across the USA during the 1960s. However, on 13 November, 1967, he came to Newcastle University, the sole reason for a 24-hour visit to Britain. King was there to receive an honorary degree, becoming an Honorary Doctor of Civil Law. During his acceptance speech, he spoke of his fight for racial equality, stating that 'the world will never rise to its full moral or political or even social maturity until racism is totally eradicated'. This was the last public address King would give outside the USA. On 4 April, 1968, he was assassinated in Memphis, Tennessee. A eulogy for King was read by the University's Vice-Chancellor Charles Bosanquet 22 days later.

King's statue was unveiled on 13 November, 2017, to commemorate the 50th anniversary of King's degree ceremony. Fittingly, it was unveiled by Ambassador Andrew Young, a close friend of King, who was with him in Newcastle.

Address Armstrong Quad, Newcastle University, Newcastle, NE1 7RU, www.ncl.ac.uk |
Getting there Bus 10, 11, 47, X 47 or X 77 and various others to Claremont Road – Museum;
Metro to Haymarket (Yellow or Green Line) | Hours Viewable during term time only |
Tip The Trent House is a pub close to the Newcastle University campus. Comfortable and
friendly with a wide choice of beers and spirits, the pub also has a 'World Famous' jukebox
that's free to use (1–2 Leazes Lane, Newcastle, NE1 4QT, +44 (0)191 261 2154).

54 Master Mariners' Homes

Hyem sweet hyem

After a hard life at sea, a sailor in the early 19th century could have been forgiven for wanting to spend his twilight years in dry, comfortable surroundings. In 1829, this cheery prospect became more likely when a group of Tyneside Masters created a Friendly Society to provide pensions to Master Mariners once they reached 60, or were injured and unable to work (a Master Mariner being a sailor qualified to be in charge of a boat or ship).

This far-sighted act was followed by the building of a retirement home for elderly Master Mariners. Land in Tynemouth was donated by Hugh Percy, 3rd Duke of Northumberland, and in 1837 the foundation stone for the new building was laid down. Finished in a Jacobean style with a central clock tower bearing the arms of Trinity House, Newcastle, the building was designed by the father and son team of John and Benjamin Green, who also worked on Grey's Monument (see ch. 34). At the top of the entrance steps is a statue of Hugh Percy, created by the sculptor Christopher Tate, as an acknowledgement of his contribution.

When the home opened in 1840 it was initially known as the Master Mariners' Asylum, and provided accommodation for Master Mariners and their dependents. In 1902, the original Friendly Society merged with the Tyne Mariners Institute to create the Tyne Mariners Benevolent Institution, now a registered charity. Since that time, the institution has managed the building, though under the less emotive name of the Master Mariners' Homes. There are currently 30 flats for needy sailors, who no longer need to be Master Mariners, but who must be 55 or over, or be unable to work, and have served at least five years at sea. Happily, the widows of qualifying seafarers are also able to apply. New tenants undergo a short period of assessment to ensure they will fit into what is said to be a happy – and a dry and comfortable – community.

Address Tynemouth Road, Tynemouth, NE30 4AS | **Getting there** Bus 1A/1B Coaster to Tynemouth Road–Rodney Close; Metro to Tynemouth (Yellow Line) | **Hours** Viewable from the outside only | **Tip** The Glasshouse Tea Room, located in the visitor centre of nearby Northumberland Park, serves a hearty range of hot food and drink throughout the year.

55 Millennium Bridge
Tilting in the blink of an eye

A joke briefly tickled Geordie funny bones a few years ago: What European town has the same number of bridges as Newcastle? The answer is of course, Gateshead. There are now seven bridges that link the two towns, with the 2000 Millennium Bridge being the newest. (Or *Gateshead* Millennium Bridge to use its full name, it being a Gateshead Council project, not a Newcastle one.)

The bridge can be used by both pedestrians and cyclists, and was the first – and so far only – bridge in the world designed to tilt. Hydraulic rams, moved by energy-efficient electric motors, push the 850-tonne steel structure into position; the whole process taking just over four minutes to complete. Concrete foundations to a depth of 98 feet help to anchor the bridge to the ground, and counteract forces generated as the bridge moves. When fully raised, the 40° tilt allows boats up to 82 feet in height to pass safely underneath. Because of the tilting, and the flattened c-shapes of the walkway and support arch, the bridge is also known as the 'Blinking Eye bridge'.

In short, the Millennium Bridge is an engineering marvel. But that is not all. Thousands of people cross the bridge every day, inevitably leaving litter behind. Rather than dropping into the Tyne as the bridge rises, the litter falls into special traps at each end. (Gates, closed once the bridge is emptied of traffic, also prevent people – even litterbugs – from plunging into the river.)

The Millennium Bridge has won many awards, including the Royal Institute of British Architects' Stirling Prize. It has also featured on stamps, and on television. In 2007, the bridge represented England on the £1 coin, in a series depicting bridges in the four countries of the United Kingdom. Thanks to those efficient motors, only four such coins would be needed to pay for the electricity used to raise the bridge. There may even be change.

Why – blinking – aye, pet.

Address Baltic Square, Gateshead, NE8 3BA, www.gateshead.gov.uk | Getting there
Bus Q1 or Q2 Quaylink to Baltic Square, or bus Q3 QuayCity to The Swirle | Hours The
Millennium Bridge usually tilts at least once a day, with the scheduled times posted in the
glass canopies at either end of the bridge. | Tip On the Newcastle side, the Millennium
Bridge leads almost directly to the entrance of the Pitcher and the Piano pub. Food is served
all day, and there is an extensive range of beers, lagers and cocktails.

56 Mining Institute

Underground overground

It is hard now to imagine what the life of a coal miner was like in the early 19th century. Mining was cruel, back-breaking work with disaster an ever-present possibility. The most feared danger was firedamp, a mix of flammable gases found in mines. One of the worst disasters of the time was the explosion at Felling Colliery on 25 May, 1812. On that dreadful day, 92 men and boys were killed.

Other disasters followed, leading to such innovations as the Miners' Safety Lamp. Then, on 3 July, 1852, after a recent explosion at Seaton Colliery, 44 coal mine owners from across the north east met to discuss the issue of safety. At the meeting at the Coal Trade Offices in Newcastle it was decided that a society should be formed. The purpose of the society was to find ways of properly ventilating mines and preventing accidents, and to discuss the 'winning and working of collieries'.

The inaugural address was given on 3 September, 1852 by the elected chairman and first president, Nicholas Wood. At the meeting the society was officially named 'The North of England Institute of Mining Engineers', becoming the 'The North of England Institute of Mining and Mechanical Engineers' in 1870. In continuous existence since then, the Institute is now the world's oldest professional mining organisation.

Initially, meetings of the Institute were held in the Lit & Phil on Westgate Road. After receiving a bequest of £2,000 following the death of engineer Robert Stephenson in 1859, plans were drawn up to build a more permanent home. The ornate high-Gothic building, named Neville Hall, was completed in 1872 and has been the home of the Institute ever since.

The centrepiece of Neville Hall is the Wood Memorial Hall, which houses the largest coal mining library in the world. Pride of place in the hall is a statue of Nicholas Wood, still keeping a careful watch over proceedings.

Address Neville Hall, Westgate Road, Newcastle, NE1 1SE, +44 (0)191 250 9717, mininginstitute.org.uk | **Getting there** Bus 1, 30 or 31 to Central Station Neville Street; Metro to Central Station (Yellow or Green Line) | **Hours** The Institute hosts regular talks and events; check website for programme | **Tip** The Dog and Scone on Pudding Chare, just a 2-minute walk from Neville Hall, is ideal for dog lovers. There you can enjoy a selection of teas, coffees and cakes in the company of the café's resident dogs (dogandscone.com).

57 Mosley Street
Let there be light!

Arguments can last minutes, days or, if you are very unlucky, several centuries, even when the cause is relatively simple. Take the humble incandescent light bulb, for example. Devised in the late-19th century, there are two contenders for the title of inventor, and this has led to a difference of opinion over primacy ever since. In the American corner is Thomas Edison, who patented his electric bulb in 1879. However, if you are British, then Sunderland-born physicist and chemist Joseph Swan is the man to champion.

Swan was born in 1828 and was, it has to be said, something of an overachiever. His interest in both chemistry and photography led him to develop both the dry photographic plate and bromide paper, the latter still in use today. In 1850, he began to experiment with creating an electric light by passing a current through a carbonised paper filament mounted in a glass jar. To lengthen the life of the filament, Swan removed as much of the air from the jar as possible. Initially unsuccessful, he then sat down and created his own vacuum pump to do the job.

After further experimentation, Swan eventually produced a working bulb that, on 3 February, 1879, was successfully demonstrated at Newcastle's Lit & Phil. Notable world firsts promptly followed. Underhill, Swan's house in Gateshead, was fitted out with his bulbs to become the first private house to be lit this way. In 1880, the library of the Lit & Phil was the first public room lit by electric light. And then there is Mosley Street. On the same evening as his Lit & Phil lecture, one of Swan's bulbs was placed inside a gas lamp on the street. The proceedings cheered on by an enthusiastic crowd, a current was then applied to the bulb. Although the light would have been feeble compared with a modern streetlamp, Mosley Street was indisputably the first street in the world illuminated by electric lighting.

Address Mosley Street, Newcastle, NE1 1DE | Getting there Bus Q2/Q3 Quaylink to Grey Street | Tip Portofino is an authentic Italian restaurant housed in the splendour of a Victorian Grade II-listed building designed by the noted architect Alfred Waterhouse (12A Mosley Street, Newcastle, NE1 1DE, +44 (0)191 261 5512, www.portofinonewcastle.co.uk).

58 Newcastle Castle

The Normans make a statement

William the Conqueror has a mixed reputation in the north. In the debit column there's the near genocidal subjugation of the region in 1069–70, when villages were burnt to the ground and thousands were brutally slaughtered. On the positive side of the ledger is the fact that, without the Norman invasion, Newcastle would now be called Monkchester.

The new castle, from which the city gets its name, was built in 1080 by Robert Curthose, eldest son of William. This was a wooden structure, built above the River Tyne. Robert's castle was an expression of pure power, intended to discourage revolt by unruly northerners, as well as providing a secure defence against possible Scottish attacks.

Wood, of course, doesn't last: it rots and is easily set on fire. This makes it less than ideal as a material with which to build a stronghold. So, between 1168 and 1178, the old new castle was replaced by one built of stone, on the orders of Henry II and at the eye-watering cost of £1,144.

Of course, even stone is not immune to the depredations of time. Today, the only part of Henry's castle still standing is the Keep, the handiwork of 'Maurice the Engineer'. When first built, the Keep was an austere rectangular affair, plain but imposing. By the 17th century the Keep was in a poor state. It was repaired during the English Civil War, but after hostilities ceased it gradually fell into disrepair again. By the late 18th century the Keep lacked a roof and was under threat of conversion into a windmill for 'the purpose of grinding Corn and Bolting Flour'.

In 1810, Newcastle Corporation bought the Keep for £630. The Keep's fancy battlements were added not long after this. Today, the Keep is open as a visitor attraction. However, marvellous though the interior is, arguably the most thrilling experience is to be had on the – now replaced – roof, with its 360° view of Monk… Newcastle.

Address Castle Garth, Newcastle, NE1 1RQ, +44 (0)191 230 6300,
www.newcastlecastle.co.uk | Getting there Bus 27 Crusader, 56 Cityrider, 57 Citylink,
58 Citylink and various others to High Level Bridge North End | Hours Thu–Mon
10am–5pm | Tip A civilised way to end a visit to Newcastle Castle is to call into the nearby
Vermont Hotel to have afternoon tea in the hotel's Redwood Bar (Vermont Hotel, Castle
Garth, Newcastle, NE1 1RQ, +44 (0)191 233 1010, www.vermont-hotel.com).

59 Newcastle Central Station

The train now arriving...

Newcastle's Central Station is the one and only railway station in the city. Given Newcastle's railway heritage, it's just as well it's a good one. It was opened on 29 August, 1850 by Queen Victoria and Prince Albert, the couple having stopped off in Newcastle on the way to a holiday on Deeside. Unfortunately, the station was far from finished. It is possible to imagine the royal couple wandering round the train shed, politely ignoring the work still to be done. It wasn't until 1863 that the main entrance portico was completed, by which time Albert had been dead for two years.

This embarrassing situation was largely the fault of one man: George Hudson. In the 1840s Hudson was the 'Railway King' controlling long stretches of the railway network. In 1846, he backed an ambitious plan to build a portico for the Central Station that would stretch the entire length of the station.

Unfortunately, Hudson's railway empire was about to come crashing down. His fall came when it was discovered that dividends in his companies were paid to shareholders using invested capital rather than profits. He was also found to be borrowing money at crippling interest rates to stay solvent. Hudson was finished when investors realised that heavy losses were imminent. After Hudson's disgrace, plans for the portico had to be revised and scaled back drastically. When built, the portico was far more modest than originally intended.

Despite all these problems, the station was a technological marvel when finished. It shares joint honour with Liverpool's Lime Street Station for the first use of curved wrought iron ribs to support an arched roof. And, though shorter than first planned, the portico is handsome and elegantly proportioned. Renovation work completed in 2014 has even improved it, making it light and airy, fitting a 19th-century structure to the needs of the 21st-century traveller.

Address Neville Street, Newcastle, NE1 5DL | **Getting there** Bus 10, 11 or 38 to Central Station Neville Street; Metro to Central Station (Yellow or Green Line); paid parking at Newcastle Station Car Park | **Tip** Tanfield Railway is a volunteer-run heritage railway attraction. Steam trains regularly run on a 6-mile round trip that crosses over the world's oldest railway bridge (Tanfield Railway, Marley Hill Engine Shed, Gateshead, NE16 5ET, +44 (0)7508 092365, www.tanfield-railway.co.uk).

60_ Old Eldon Square

Out with the old and in with the new

1976 was an exciting time to be a shopper in Newcastle. This was the year that the Eldon Square Shopping Centre opened to the public, offering the futuristic thrill of an American-style mall in the centre of the city. Unfortunately, progress comes at a price and nowhere is this more poignantly visible than in Old Eldon Square.

Turn slowly round in the square and you'll notice that the architecture is an odd mix of styles. Two sides of the square are formed by the blandly modern façade of Eldon Square. The east side of the square is a Palladian-style terrace, and which very obviously pre-dates the shopping centre. Old Eldon Square was designed by Thomas Oliver, and was part of Richard Grainger's extensive redevelopment of Newcastle city centre in the 1820s (see ch. 33). Completed in 1831, the square was named after the first Earl of Eldon, better known as John Scott, who eloped with Bessie Surtees in 1772 (see ch. 7). Originally there were three sides to the terrace, providing 25 homes in total. At the heart of the square was a private garden for the residents. This was opened to the public in the 1920s after a World War I memorial was erected at its centre.

In 1963, a development plan set out a number of proposals to increase the space for shopping in the city, one of which called for the demolition of Old Eldon Square. Planning was granted, though not without controversy. Richard Crossman, Minister for Housing and Local Government in 1965, was a particular critic of the decision, describing Old Eldon Square as 'a beautiful Georgian Square, which they were going to destroy for a shopping centre…'. Ultimately, the third side was only saved because permission to demolish a non-conformist chapel behind the terrace was refused by the Secretary of State. So now Newcastle has a one-sided square, a strange relic of an earlier and less frenetic time. It's not much, but one side is better than none at all.

Address Blackett Street, Newcastle, NE1 7JG | **Getting there** Bus 12, 32, 32A, 62,
63 or X63 to Newcastle Monument; Metro to Monument (Yellow or Green Line) | **Tip**
Mr Wolf is a family-run independent toy shop on Old Eldon Square selling a range of toys,
games and puzzles for children of all ages (5–6 Old Eldon Square, Newcastle, NE1 7JG,
+44 (0)191 222 1567, www.mrwolf.uk.com).

61 Original Penny Bazaar
Small but perfectly formed

The Grainger Market is an architectural gem at the heart of New-castle. It is a 19th-century covered market hall, and a rare example in the UK of one still used for its original purpose. Shopping in the Grainger Market is a rite of passage for any self-respecting Geordie, or indeed for anyone keen to find a bargain. However, there is one shop that really cannot be missed. It is the Marks & Spencer Original Penny Bazaar – the world's smallest M&S and the only original M&S Penny Bazaar still trading.

The story of M&S begins with Micheal Marks, a Jewish refugee from Belarus who, after arriving in northern England, worked as a pedlar. Despite the handicap of his poor English, he thrived and was soon running a stall in Kirkgate Market in Leeds. Goods were arranged by price on the stall and Marks quickly discovered that the penny section was the most popular. (Cannily, Marks used the slo-gan 'Don't ask the price, it's a penny' to catch shoppers' attention.) Realising he was on to a good thing, Marks concentrated solely on high-quality and useful goods – buttons, soap, wool – that could profitably be sold for a penny.

Needing a partner to expand his business, Marks approached Isaac Dewhirst who had previously loaned him money. Dewhirst wasn't interested but did recommend his senior cashier, Tom Spencer. Happily, Spencer agreed to invest £300 in the business. The partnership formed, Marks and Spencer officially started trading on 28 September, 1894.

Newcastle's Penny Bazaar was opened in 1895 and has been a fixture in the Grainger Market ever since. Although the original gas lamps are now lit by electricity, the frontage is so authentic and carefully preserved that a time-traveller from the 1890s would find it all reassuringly familiar. The only thing that might shock the chron-onaut are the 21st-century prices. A penny really doesn't go as far as it once did.

Address Units 133–138, Grainger Market, Grainger Street, Newcastle, NE1 5QQ |
Getting there Bus 1A Coaster, 1B Coaster, 22 or 22X to Monument Grainger Street; Metro
Monument (Yellow or Green Line) | **Hours** Mon–Sat 9am–5.30pm | **Tip** The Pet Lamb
Patisserie in the Grainger Market sells a wide range of traybakes, freshly made each day
(Unit 19, Grainger Market, Grainger Street, Newcastle, NE1 5QF).

62 Ouseburn Jetty
Bob and Terry revisited

The 1970s was arguably a golden era for British sitcoms. One of the hits of 1973 was *Whatever Happened to the Likely Lads?*, written by Dick Clement and Ian La Frenais. Set on Tyneside, the premise was simple: work-shy Terry Collier (James Bolam) returns home to the north east having spent five years in the British Army, stationed in Germany. On the train home to Newcastle, Terry bumps into his friend Bob Ferris (Rodney Bewes), whom he hasn't spoken to since joining the army. The intervening years have changed Bob, who now aspires to join the middle class with his fiancé, later wife, Thelma (Brigit Forsyth).

The return of Terry causes tension with Thelma, whose thin-lipped disapproval of his working-class manners drives much of the comedy. Over the course of two series, Bob and Terry get into various comedic scrapes together. Between the laughs, however, they also find time to ruminate with a wistful regret on the changes wrought by the passing of the years.

Like most sitcoms of the time, the show was largely filmed in a studio, watched by a live audience. However, the opening credits and the occasional outdoor scene were shot on location in Newcastle. To modern eyes this gives the show a strangely documentary feel. Newcastle was in flux at the time, as serious redevelopment of the city was underway. Nowhere is this change more apparent than at the mouth of the Ouseburn. This location was used in both the opening credits and in series two, when Terry says goodbye to Susan, Thelma's sister, who is returning home to Canada. The two stand on a jetty against an industrial backdrop of warehouses and cranes busily loading cargo ships. This scene has completely changed. No longer industrial, pleasure boats have replaced the ships, and in the distance are swanky new riverside apartments instead of warehouses. Terry would be appalled, but Bob and Thelma would surely approve.

Address Quayside, Newcastle, NE6 1BU | Getting there Bus Q3 QuayCity to Walker Road–Horatio Street; Metro to Manors (Yellow Line), then a 19-minute walk; free parking at Spiller's Car Park | Tip The Cycle Hub on Quayside is a bicycle repair shop where you can also hire bikes for periods of one hour up to 14 days. There is also a café on-site selling simple but wholesome food and drink (+44 (0)191 276 7250, www.thecyclehub.org).

63 Ouseburn Street Art

Stepney Banksies

The Lower Ouseburn Valley has seen many changes over the centuries. Originally agricultural, this changed once the Industrial Revolution began to heat up on Tyneside. Initially it was glass and pottery manufacturing that took hold in the valley. Over the course of the 19th century, other industries followed, including warehousing and mills, and lead works to produce white paint.

With factories came a need for workers' housing. As a consequence, the valley was one of the first industrial suburbs in Newcastle. The key was the Ouseburn itself, which provided a useful water source, as well as easy access to the River Tyne for the delivery of raw materials and the shipping of finished goods. All this industry in such a relatively small area ultimately had a cost, however. The environment degraded over time with the Ouseburn itself becoming heavily polluted. Housing conditions were squalid too, with families living cheek by jowl in cramped conditions. Change first came in the 1930s with a series of slum clearance programmes. And then, in the 1950s, industry in the valley began a long slow decline.

What could have been terminal proved to be a chance for reinvention, starting with the renovation of The Cluny warehouse in the 1980s (see ch. 20). Since 1995, the Ouseburn Trust has overseen the development of the valley as a creative community and leisure district, with old industrial buildings repurposed and modern housing built. Perhaps the most tangible sign of how the character of the valley has evolved is the dazzling variety of murals and street art painted on buildings and bridges. The art ranges from the pictorial – such as the huge sheep's face on the Ship Inn, painted by Unit 44 and American artist Gaia – to the abstract. The smaller examples of street art come and go, so change is constant – rather fittingly just like the history of the Lower Ouseburn Valley. This all means that there's always something new to see.

Address Stepney Bank, Ouseburn, Newcastle, NE1 2PW | Getting there Bus 12, 39 or 40 to New Bridge Street–Blackfriars, then a 5-minute walk | Tip The Tyne Bar is an independent pub and live music venue. Food is served every day, with a varied menu that caters to all tastes, including options for vegans (1 Maling Street, Newcastle, NE6 1LP, +44 (0) 265 2550, www.thetyne.com).

64 Palace of Arts

Party on like it's 1929!

It is common knowledge that Geordies like a celebratory knees-up. The biggest jamboree in Newcastle's history was held on a corner of the Town Moor that has forever afterwards been known as Exhibition Park. Apart from this name change, the only other evidence for this event is the Palace of Arts.

The 1929 North East Coast Exhibition was opened on 14 May, 1929 by the then Prince of Wales, later King Edward VIII. The exhibition was organised to promote industry on Tyneside to a wider world, industry that was in decline after the peak years of World War I. By the time the exhibition closed on 26 October, 1929, over four million people had paid a visit, at an average of 30,000 visitors per day.

The Exhibition site was 50 hectares in size, most of which was devoted to garden displays. Unusually for the time, the job of Director of Horticulture was awarded to a woman, a Miss Kelly. To house the various exhibits, new buildings were constructed, mainly in the Art Deco style of the day. By far the largest of these buildings were the Palaces of Engineering and Industries. The first housed scale models showcasing the products of Tyneside's heavy industries. Strangely, despite the name, the Palace of Industries was largely filled with displays of consumer products, including Newcastle Exhibition Ale and, coincidentally or not, Andrews Liver Salts.

The Palace of Arts was tiny in comparison. It was used to house over 300 works of art, and was the only building designed to be a permanent structure. Unfortunately, thanks to a problem of inadequate ventilation, some of the art developed mildew. After the Exhibition, the park was cleared and the art removed from the Palace of Arts, which became Newcastle's Science Museum. The museum has since been relocated and renamed Discovery; here you can find a permanent and informative exhibit on the oh-so temporary Exhibition.

Address Palace of Arts, Exhibition Park, Newcastle, NE2 4PZ | **Getting there** Bus 30, 31 or 35 and various others to Great North Road – Clayton Road; paid parking at Claremont Road Car Park, then an 11-minute walk | **Tip** The Palace of Arts is now home to Wylam Brewery, who produce craft beers for local pubs. Wylam Brewery regularly run tours so you can see how the beer is made and view the interior of the building (www.wylambrewery.co.uk).

65 Pedestrian Tyne Tunnel
Stairway to Hebburn

As rivers go, the Tyne isn't that spectacular. Compared with the Amazon or Nile it's a mere trickle. It's not even the longest river in the United Kingdom, languishing a lowly 24th on the league table. However, this doesn't make the Tyne any easier to cross, particularly at its eastern extremes where a bridge is impracticable.

In the 1920s, a proposal to build a tunnel between North and South Shields was considered. This was to feature high-speed electric monorail cars that would whizz passengers back and forth. Sadly, this thrillingly futuristic idea was abandoned. Then, in 1937, a scheme to build three tunnels under the Tyne was agreed upon. One tunnel would be used for vehicles, the other two, which would run side-by-side, for pedestrians and cyclists.

World War II interrupted these plans, but they were revived in 1947 when work began on the pedestrian and cyclist tunnels. As these were smaller than the proposed vehicle tunnel, they were cheaper to build and so were started first. (Work on the vehicle tunnel eventually started in 1961.) On 24 July, 1951, the tunnels were opened by Transport Minister Alfred Barnes. On the day, Barnes would probably have ridden on one of the tunnel's wooden escalators, which, at 197 feet long, are the longest wooden escalators in the UK.

At the peak of their use, over 20,000 people used the tunnels daily. These were typically workers, off to the shipyards and factories then found along the Tyne. As industry on Tyneside declined so did use of the tunnels. By the 21st century daily usage had dropped to fewer than 700 people. In 2000, the tunnels were granted Grade II-listed status as a structure of special historical interest. And then, in 2013, an extensive restoration of the tunnels began, culminating in a grand reopening on 7 August, 2019. Wonderfully, you can still ride those same escalators down into the depths. An electric monorail is unfortunately still unlikely.

Address Wallsend, NE28 0PD (north entrance) or Jarrow, NE32 3PS (south entrance) |
Getting there Bus 11 Little Coasters to Bewicke Street–Coach Open (north entrance) or
bus 27 Crusader to Pedestrian Tunnel (south entrance); Metro to Howden (Yellow Line),
then a 13-minute walk (north entrance) or Jarrow (Yellow Line), then a 15-minute walk |
Tip Sambuca is a budget-friendly Italian restaurant just 5-minutes' walk from the north
entrance of the pedestrian tunnel (Northumberland Dock Road, Wallsend, NE28 6ST,
+44 (0)191 263 7799, sambucarestaurants.co.uk).

66 Quayside Chimneys
Home is where the hearth is

Stand on the Newcastle side of the Tyne Bridge and face east. From this lofty vantage point, looking across the rooftops of the city, you could spend hours just counting chimneys. You are in the right place if you need proof of how important coal once was.

Coal is a sedimentary rock formed by decaying plant matter, turned solid by pressure, heat and a vast amount of time. The northern coal seams of Northumberland and County Durham formed 309–312 million years ago during the Westphalian Stage of the Carboniferous Period. At this point in pre-history, what became northern England was more equatorial than it currently is, with a warm and wet climate. The trees that formed the coal grew in swampland in great swathes of rain forest. Splitting a lump of coal occasionally reveals the fossil evidence of these forests in the delicate tracing of leaves or in the rough bark of a Lepidodendron.

Initially coal was collected on beaches. Sea coal, washed in by the tide, was easy to find but hard work to collect in quantity. By the 13th century, coal was mined from shallow seams along the banks of the River Tyne. However, increasing demand for coal required digging deeper. The first deep pit in the region was Hetton Colliery, sunk in 1821. At a depth of 985 feet, it was an outstanding technological achievement for an age that still relied on candlelight for illumination. To transport the coal on to Sunderland, the owners employed George Stephenson to design a railway system. The result was the first railway that did not rely on animal power to pull the wagons, but on steam locomotives developed by Stephenson.

Today, a new building is more likely to have a solar panel on the roof than a chimney. And since turning smokeless in 1993, Newcastle is a far cleaner and fresher place. But there are undoubtedly those who still miss the cheery glow of a real coal fire.

Old King Coal is dead, but not forgotten.

Address Newcastle, NE1 3AE | Getting there Bus Q1/Q3 Quaylink to Quayside Guildhall | Tip Woodhorn Museum is located in Ashington, once the largest pit village in the world. A particular highlight is the Ashington Group Collection Gallery, showing artwork by the amateur 'Pitmen Painters' from the village (Woodhorn Museum, Queen Elizabeth II Country Park, Ashington, NE63 9YF, +44 (0)1670 624 455, museumsnorthumberland.org.uk).

67 Quayside Market
Open-air bargains

Newcastle is a mercantile city, the evidence for which can be seen in the number of streets named after markets: Groat Market (where oats were sold), Bigg Market (where you could buy bigg, a type of coarse barley), and Cloth Market, to name just three. None of these streets has markets now, and yet the names have stuck. Ironically, the one regular market that still exists – the Quayside Market, held every Sunday – *hasn't* left a mark in the form of a permanent street name.

This is odd, because the Quayside Market has a very long history. Its first recorded occurrence was in 1736, but it's likely that it was held for centuries before this date. In the 18th century, the market stretched from the old Tyne Bridge (where the Swing Bridge is today) along to Sandgate (near the Millennium Bridge). It's thought that the pulling down of the old town walls (see ch. 106) on the river helped to increase the size and popularity of the market. Unlike today's market, there would have been a variety of other distractions then, from fairground rides and attractions to racing tipsters. These days you're more likely to find a *cappuccino*.

Memories of the sheer showmanship of the market's 20th-century traders live on. One woman interviewed for the *Evening Chronicle* remembered a man selling crockery who 'never stopped talking about his wares. When he came to the plates and saucers he'd juggle them in the air, talking all the time.' Thanks to falling attendance in the early 2000s there was a danger that the market would cease. Fortunately, the market survived and is once again flourishing. Sadly, there are fewer theatrics on display now. However, there *is* a wide range of tempting goods on sale, from locally made crafts to second-hand books, and exotic foods from Europe and beyond to traditional northern fare. Though you will struggle to find oats and barley, unless you buy muesli.

Address Quayside, Newcastle, NE1 3DE | Getting there Bus Q2/Q3 Quaylink to Quayside Guildhall | Hours Sun 9am–4pm | Tip The Broad Chare is a proper pub, selling craft beers including 'The Writer's Block', brewed specially for the pub by Wylam Brewery (25 Broad Chare, Newcastle, NE1 3DQ, +44 (0)191 211 2144, www.thebroadchare.co.uk).

68 Renforth Monument

Sculling skill

The importance of sporting heroes isn't a modern phenomenon. The Renforth Monument outside the Shipley Art Gallery pays tribute to one of the north east's great sportsmen. However, rather than show a moment of triumph it commemorates an altogether more tragic event.

James Renforth was born in Newcastle in 1842 and spent his childhood in Pipewellgate, Gateshead. He grew up to be a strapping young man, who, after a short spell serving with the army in India, became a waterman who ferried workers out to the old Newcastle Bridge during its demolition (see ch. 90). This experience gave him the raw stamina to compete in and win his first sculling competition in 1866. Then, at a regatta on the Thames in 1868, Renforth beat the Londoner Henry Kelley by four lengths. He was crowned World Champion and won a – then huge – prize of £90.

After this, Renforth found that potential contenders were unwilling to race against him. Competitive rowing still called though, and so Renforth started racing in pairs and fours rather than solo. It was with a team that Renforth travelled to Canada in 1871, accepting a challenge to race a crew from Saint John, Brunswick. On the team was Renforth's erstwhile rival, Kelley, who was now a friend.

At 7am on 23 August the teams began the six-mile race on the Kennebecasis River. The English team were in the lead when Renforth collapsed into the lap of the man behind him – the scene depicted on the monument, with a bearded Kelley cradling Renforth. Calling to Kelley, his last words were 'What will they say in England?' Brought to shore, he was pronounced dead. What caused Renforth's death is still a mystery. Scurrilous rumours circulated that he'd been poisoned. However, the most likely explanation is heart failure following an epileptic fit. Over 100,000 people attended his funeral in Gateshead, there to mourn the loss of a true sporting hero.

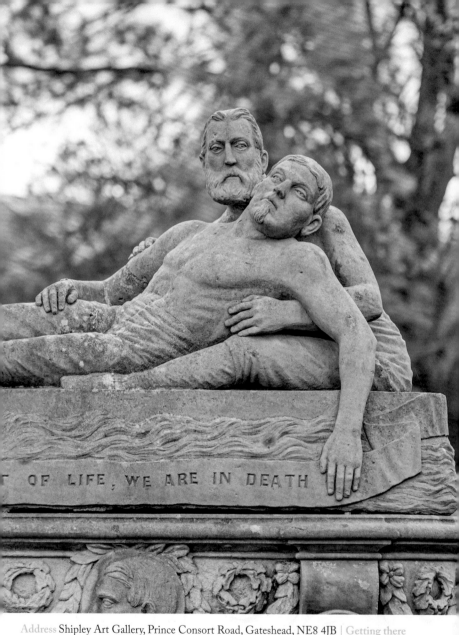

T OF LIFE, WE ARE IN DEATH

Address Shipley Art Gallery, Prince Consort Road, Gateshead, NE8 4JB | Getting there
Bus Q2 Quaylink, S844 to Prince Consort Road–Shipcote Lane, or bus 21 Angel, 25 or
28B to Durham Road–Northbourne Street; Metro to Gateshead (Yellow or Green Line),
then a 16-minute walk; free parking to a maximum of 3 hours at Prince Consort Road Car
Park | Tip Saltwell Park Model Boat Club members sail their boats on nearby Saltwell
Park's Boating Lake all year round every Saturday and Sunday (9am–1pm) and Wednesday
(noon–3pm during the winter months, 10am–7.30pm in summer).

ERECTED

69 The Response

Not for self, but for country

The declaration of war on 4 August, 1914 caused Sir Edward Grey, British Foreign Secretary, to gloomily remark that, 'The lamps are going out all over Europe, we shall not see them lit again in our life-time.' Across Britain, however, the news created a swell of patriotic fervour. Men in villages, towns and cities across the country immediately rushed to enlist. After all, it would be a once-in-a-lifetime chance for foreign adventure, and one that would likely be over by Christmas.

The Response is a poignant portrayal of a time in the early years of World War I, when enthusiasm for enlisting was still high. It captures the events of April 1915, when the men of the 5th Battalion Northumberland Fusiliers marched from their camp in Gosforth, through the Haymarket to the Central Station. From there, transport would take them on to the battlefields of France and Belgium, to take part in the Battles of Ypres, the Somme and Passchendaele.

The Battalion's march through Newcastle appears to have been a joyous occasion, with a drummer boy leading the column, and men, women and children lining the streets to cheer the soldiers on their way. However, by the early 1920s there was more pain than joy at the memory of what became known as the Great War. One man who had reason to be grateful, however, was Sir George Renwick, whose five sons all survived wartime service. It was Renwick, MP for Newcastle Central, who commissioned *The Response* as a memorial to those less fortunate. Designed by Sir William Goscombe John RA, *The Response* was officially dedicated by HRH The Prince of Wales on 5 July, 1923, before a massed gathering of spectators and a guard of honour from the Northumberland Fusiliers. Since then, *The Response* has been the focus for gatherings of remembrance every 11 November for those lost in the War to End All Wars, and in all the wars that followed.

Address St Mary's Place, Newcastle, NE1 7PF | **Getting there** Bus 10, 43, 44, 45 Sapphire, 46, 47, X14, X30 and various others to Haymarket Barras Bridge; Metro to Haymarket (Yellow or Green Line) | **Tip** *The Response* is in the grounds of the Church of St Thomas the Martyr. A Victorian building, legend has it that an older chapel of the same name was founded by Hugh de Morville as penance for his role in the assassination of Thomas Becket.

70 RGS Pillar

The humble beginnings of a northern institution

The Royal Grammar School, or RGS, is a prestigious independent school. The RGS's current home in Jesmond is a gleaming state-of-the-art facility, with all the amenities a child could ask for. However, just a mile away (as the crow flies) is a small reminder of the school's earliest days.

Walk briskly around the final curve of Westgate Road, just before it reaches Neville Street, and you risk bumping into a single stone pillar. Incongruously situated next to a modern extension of The Head of Steam pub, the pillar was once part of a gateway into the Hospital of St Mary the Virgin. Built in the 12th century, the hospital was not a hospital in the sense we understand today, but was there 'to serve God and the poor, and to be a place of entertainment for the indigent clergy and such pilgrims as are passing this way'.

In 1607, the hospital's chapel was given over to the Free Grammar School, later to become the RGS. Founded in 1545, and then attended by boys only, the school originally occupied a building in the churchyard of St Nicholas' Cathedral. In 1844, the buildings of the hospital and school were pulled down in order to allow the redevelopment of Neville Street in anticipation of the building of Newcastle's Central Station. With the odd exception of the solitary pillar, that is. The school moved on to new premises before finally settling in its present location in 1906.

One tradition that arose during the school's time in the chapel came about when the hospital's chancel was turned into an election house for the selection of the town's mayor and civic officers. On 29 September every year the new mayor would collect his staff of office from an oak table in the chancel. In celebration, the boys of the school would be given the day off. The tradition of the Lord Mayor's Holiday is still practised at the RGS, now in the first week of December.

Address Westgate Road, Newcastle, NE1 5EN | **Getting there** Bus 10, 11 or 38 to Central
Station Neville Street; Metro to Central Station (Yellow or Green Line) | **Tip** The Victorian
Comet pub on Neville Street serves Irish-influenced food and drink. The pub appears in the
classic movie *Get Carter* and is the first place Jack Carter, played by Michael Caine, visits
after he arrives in Newcastle.

71 River Tyne

It's clean-up time

The River Tyne has a split personality, starting as two rivers not one. The River South Tyne starts its journey in the hills of the North Pennines. By a geographical quirk, two of the north east's other rivers – the Wear and the Tees – have their source in this same area. The River North Tyne flows from hills near the village of Kielder, not far from the Scottish Borders. The two rivers meet north west of Hexham, flowing east from there to Tyneside and the North Sea.

The river changes character as it reaches Tyneside, and once not necessarily for the better. Last century the Tyne was highly polluted, and thought to be one of the dirtiest in the country. In 1958, Irene Ward, MP for Tynemouth, declared in the House of Commons that 'the condition of the river is deplorable and intolerable'.

There were many causes, from the pollutants of industry and farming to domestic waste flowing into the river. Salmon are a good indicator of a river's health. The fish was once so common in the Tyne that apprentices and servants often had agreements with their employers to limit the number of salmon-themed meals served. By the 1950s, however, the water quality in the Tyne was so poor that salmon had all but vanished.

Today, the Tyne is a far cleaner river, thanks to work by organisations such as the Tyne Rivers Trust, the region's local councils, and the Port of Tyne. Infrastructure projects have solved problems, but so has sheer hard work by volunteers willing to spend time keeping the river clean. Happily, this means that salmon have now returned. Kielder Hatchery reintroduced salmon back into the Tyne in 1979. Since then the fish have thrived and the Tyne is now considered one of the best salmon rivers in England. Which is good news for the salmon and good news for us: everyone benefits from clean rivers, particularly when a river is at the heart of a region's identity.

Address St Peter's Basin, Bottlehouse Street, Newcastle, NE6 1HX | Getting there Bus 18 or Q3 QuayCity to St Lawrence Road; Metro to Byker (Yellow Line), then a 23-minute walk; free parking on St Lawrence Road | Tip St Peter's Basin was once an industrial area on the Tyne. It's now a popular residential area with a marina and splendid views of the river. The Merchant's Tavern offers good solid English fare at reasonable prices.

72 River Tyne God

Urban Aquaman

Apparently defying gravity high above the ground on the wall of Newcastle Civic Centre is the figure of a giant, 16 feet high and weighing three and a half tons. His left hand points accusingly down to the ground, his right held high above his head. The expression on his face is unreadable. Is he angry? Sad? No matter. He is the *River Tyne God* and he probably knows where you live, so don't do anything foolish in his presence.

The *River Tyne God* is a *genius loci*, a Roman spirit who protects a particular place. Altars found across Europe often depict *genii locorum*, generally shown holding a physical symbol such as a snake or cornucopia. Despite his timeless qualities, the original *River Tyne God* was not Roman in origin, but instead dates from 1786. He was one of nine masks designed by Sir William Chambers and added to the façade of Somerset House in London. One mask represents the Ocean, each of the other eight represents a British river. In a nod to regionality, Chambers' *River Tyne God* sports a natty basket of burning coals on his head, with tools used in mining entwined in the fish that represent his hair.

Chambers' *River Tyne God* design was later engraved in copper and, in 1789, used on the frontispiece to Volume II of *The History and Antiquities of the Town and County of the Town of Newcastle Upon Tyne* by John Brand (snappy book titles weren't common in the 18th century). This engraving has been used again and again to represent the region ever since.

The Civic Centre *River Tyne God* was created by David Wynne. Completed in 1968, Wynne's *River Tyne God* does not have the burning coals or fish of the original and so has a more mythical quality. He was also once a fountain, with water cascading from his raised right hand before flowing down his body and beard. Perhaps then it is puzzlement that shows on his face, a river god wondering where the water went.

Address Newcastle Civic Centre, Newcastle, NE1 8QH | **Getting there** Bus 10, 43, 44 or 45 Sapphire, 46, 47, X14 or X30 and various others to Haymarket Barras Bridge; Metro to Haymarket (Yellow or Green Line); paid parking at Sandyford Square (Civic Centre) Car Park | **Tip** Northern Stage, just 5-minutes' walk from the Civic Centre, is a contemporary three-stage theatre showing a varied programme of in-house productions, as well as performances and plays staged by visiting companies (Barras Bridge, Newcastle, NE1 7RH, +44 (0)191 230 5151, www.northernstage.co.uk).

73 RMS *Carpathia*
Full steam ahead

It is 14 April, 1912. The Atlantic Ocean is as smooth as glass, and the night sky dusted with stars. RMS *Titanic* steams through the darkness *en route* to New York. It is her maiden voyage, and it will prove to be her last. At 11.39pm lookout Frederick Fleet spots an iceberg directly in *Titanic*'s path. Alerting the bridge, he can only watch in horror as the ship slowly – too slowly – steers to port. There is a ghastly scream of metal tearing as the iceberg scrapes along the starboard side of *Titanic*. Holed below the waterline, she slowly starts to sink.

At 00.15am the order to send a distress signal is given. *Titanic*'s radio operators, Jack Phillips and Harold Bride, begin to tap out CQD and SOS in the hope that someone, somewhere out there will hear the call. More than 58 miles distant, RMS *Carpathia* responds. On hearing the news, Arthur Rostron, the *Carpathia*'s captain, orders full steam ahead. The *Carpathia* is on her way…

The *Carpathia*'s crew is rightly held in high esteem. The Atlantic in April is cold and unforgiving. By dashing to *Titanic*'s rescue, Rostron put the *Carpathia* in danger too. That she reached her destination safely is a testament to the skill of *Carpathia*'s crew. Sadly, of course, they were too late. The *Titanic* had gone. Her cold and traumatised survivors were found sitting huddled in lifeboats, a shockingly scant 705 of the original 2,208 passengers and crew.

The *Carpathia* was built on Tyneside at the Swan Hunter shipyard, and began service in 1903. Sadly the *Carpathia* too was destined to sink, the victim of a German U-Boat attack in 1918. A wonderfully large and detailed scale model of the *Carpathia* is on display at the Segedunum Roman Fort. Ship models were commissioned by shipbuilders or ship owners to celebrate and promote their products and services. Segedunum's *Carpathia* model is a fitting tribute to the little ship that could.

Address Segedunum Roman Fort, Buddle Street, Wallsend, NE28 6HR,
+44 (0)191 278 4217, www.segedunumromanfort.org.uk | Getting there Bus 12, 41
Little Coasters, 40, 42, 42A, 553, Q3 QuayCity or 901 to Wallsend Metro, or bus 12 to
Buddle Street–Segedunum; Metro to Wallsend (Yellow Line); free on-site parking | Hours
May–Sept, daily 10am–5pm, Oct, daily 10am–4pm, Nov–Apr, Mon–Fri 10am–2.30pm |
Tip There is reconstruction of a short stretch of Hadrian's Wall near Plantation Street, just
5-minutes' walk from Segedunum.

74 Royal Arcade Columns
The best laid plans…

At the heart of the leafy splendour that is Armstrong Park are three stumpy stone columns. There are no signposts to guide you to their resting place, and there is no handy information board to explain their purpose. They sit in the shadow of the shoe tree, festooned with shoes thrown by grateful students celebrating the end of exams.

The columns were originally part of the Royal Arcade, one of the rare failures of Grainger Town (see ch. 33). The Royal Arcade was designed by the architect John Dobson and completed in 1832 at a cost of £45,000. Thrillingly modern at the time, the Royal Arcade housed shops, banks, offices, and even a steam and vapour bath. Contemporary etchings show a spaciously light and airy classically inspired interior, with a high ceiling featuring eight conical skylights to provide illumination. Unfortunately, the arcade was built in the wrong place, in an unfashionable part of Newcastle far from the bustling centre. The eastern end also opened out onto Manor Chare, which had an insalubrious reputation and was certainly no place for a fashionable lady to be seen. The Royal Arcade was ultimately a commercial disappointment. Businesses left and the building gradually fell into disuse and disrepair. In 1963 it was controversially pulled down so that Swan House could be built. And that was that.

Only… not quite. Each stone from the Royal Arcade was carefully numbered in chalk, so that, like a gigantic three-dimensional jigsaw, the arcade could be rebuilt elsewhere. For a number of years the stone was stored outside at a site in Sandyford. And then it was discovered that the numbers had long washed away. The plans to rebuild were shelved, and the stone was largely used as the foundations for roads. The three columns in Armstrong Park were spared this fate, and are a strangely poignant reminder of an architectural gem now long gone.

Address Armstrong Park, Heaton Road, Newcastle, NE6 5JT | **Getting there** Bus 18 or 18A to Heaton Road – Rothbury Terrace, parking at Jesmond Vale Lane Car Park | **Tip** The nearby Sky Apple Café serves vegetarian and vegan meals and desserts (186 Heaton Road, Heaton, NE6 5HP, +44 (0)191 276 3935, www.skyapple.co.uk).

75 Sage Gateshead

Sing a song in a decagon

If you want to split public opinion, design a modern building unlike anything seen before, placing it in a prominent place at the heart of a city. The Sage Gateshead is just such a building. Designed by Norman Foster's architectural studio and completed in 2004, it was one of the candidates for *Private Eye*'s 'Hugh Casson Medal' for the worst new building that year. More happily, the Sage was also a finalist in the Prime Minister's Better Public Building Award in 2005.

The swooping organic shape of the glass exterior has been variously described as looking like an armadillo, a seashell, and, less kindly perhaps, a giant slug. The exterior is the shape it is to 'shrink-wrap' around the three auditoria within. The largest auditorium, Sage One, can seat up to 1,700 and is typically used for orchestral performances. Seating 400, Sage Two is smaller, is believed to be the only 10-sided concert venue in the world, and is used for more intimate musical events. The third space is used as a rehearsal space for the Royal Northern Sinfonia, and to host the Sage's regular music classes and workshops. The various auditoria are all considered to be acoustically state-of the-art. This has been achieved passively through the use of specific building materials, such as a 'spongy' concrete mix, and actively through the use of floating ceiling panels that can be moved to fine-tune the soundscape.

The Sage is home to the Royal Northern Sinfonia, the 'Royal' prefix bestowed by the Queen in 2013. The Northern Sinfonia, as it was then, was founded in 1958 by Michael Hall, and originally based in Newcastle's City Hall until a move to the Sage in 2004. The Sinfonia has the distinction of being the first professional resident chamber orchestra outside London. One thing that everyone can agree on is that the Sinfonia's annual classical season is a northern cultural highlight.

Address St Mary's Square, Gateshead, NE8 2JR, +44 (0)191 443 4666, www.sagegateshead.com | **Getting there** Bus 93, 94 or Q1/Q2 Quaylink to The Sage Gateshead; paid parking at Sage Gateshead Car Park | **Hours** Daily 8.50am–11pm (on non-performance days the Sage closes 30 minutes after the last class has started) | **Tip** The Riverside is a live rock and pop venue housed in the splendidly ornate Old Fish Market building on Newcastle's quayside (Neptune House, 1 The Close, Newcastle, NE1 3RQ, www.riversidencl.co.uk).

76_Saltwell Towers

Artistic architecture fit for an artist

Saltwell Towers, in Gateshead's Saltwell Park, is an eclectic mix of Gothic, Elizabethan and French styles, and has been described as an 'eccentric castle', thanks to its asymmetrical towers and crenellated parapets. Fittingly then, the man who commissioned the building, William Wailes, was not your run-of-the-mill Victorian but an artistic entrepreneur.

Born in Newcastle, Wailes started out as a tea merchant and grocer but his real passion was art. After setting up a kiln in the back yard of his shop, Wailes began to create small decorative enamels for sale. In 1830, he travelled to Germany to study the process of designing and producing stained glass. It is a difficult subject to master, but Wailes was praised during his studies for his hard work and dedication to the art of glass production.

Back in the north east, Wailes opened a stained-glass studio in 1838, and began creating his own glass in 1841. At its height, the studio employed over 70 people and gained an enviable reputation for the beauty and colour of its products. So renowned was the studio that it was one of 25 that took part in the Great Exhibition in 1851.

In 1860, married and with a family, Wailes bought Saltwell Estate. Wailes had the grounds landscaped before work began on Saltwell Towers, which was completed in 1871. Unfortunately, by 1876, Wailes had slid into debt and was forced to sell the estate to Gateshead Corporation, though the family continued to live in Saltwell Towers until Wailes' death in 1881.

During World War I, the building was used as a hospital. Between 1933 and 1969 it housed a museum, before falling into disrepair. After extensive refurbishment, it was reopened in 2004 as a café and space for art exhibitions. Rightfully, Wailes has not been forgotten, and the centrepiece of the building is a two-storey decorative glass screen designed by glass artist Bridget Jones.

Address Saltwell Park, Gateshead, NE9 5AX | Getting there Bus 28A, 29, 68B or 69 to Saltwell Park; free parking at Saltwell Park Car Park | Hours Apr–Oct, daily 9am–5pm, Nov–Mar, daily 9am–3pm | Tip To see an example of William Wailes' ecclesiastical stained glass, visit St Helen's Church in Low Fell, Gateshead.

77 __ Seven Stories

Once upon a time...

A childhood without books would be a poor one indeed, which is as good a reason as any to give thanks for the existence of Seven Stories – the National Centre for Children's Books. It all began in 1996, when Elizabeth Hammill OBE and Mary Briggs OBE set up a charity with the aim of celebrating and promoting books written for children. At the time, original drawings and manuscripts by British authors and illustrators were being lost to collectors overseas. Creating an archive was therefore also a priority.

In 2002, the charity bought a seven-storey Victorian grain warehouse in the Lower Ouseburn Valley, then going through a long-term process of regeneration (see ch. 63). Extensive renovation resulted in the opening of Seven Stories on 19 August, 2005 by the then Children's Laureate, Jacqueline Wilson.

From the start, children's authors have supported Seven Stories. Perhaps the most prestigious contribution was the donation by Michael Morpurgo of his entire archive. This includes hand-written drafts of some of his best-known books such as *Private Peaceful* and *The Butterfly Lion*, as well as material such as drafts from the adaptation of *War Horse* to both stage and screen. The late Judith Kerr also requested that Seven Stories house her archive, from her earliest childhood drawings to artwork for classic books such as *The Tiger Who Came to Tea* and *Mog the Forgetful Cat*.

Although Seven Stories is a museum, it's also actively involved in encouraging children to read more. Schools can participate in a membership scheme, which includes school visits to exhibitions at Seven Stories. The Centre also participates in the Children's University, a Manchester-based charity that works to develop a love of learning in children through extra-curricular activities. After all, a child who wants to learn is one who has a better chance of their life story having a happy ending.

Address 30 Lime Street, Ouseburn Valley, Newcastle, NE1 2PQ, +44 (03)00 330 1095 ext. 300, www.sevenstories.org.uk | **Getting there** Bus 12, 39 or 40 to New Bridge Street – Blackfriars, then a 7-minute walk; Metro to Manors (Yellow Line), then a 14-minute walk; paid parking at the Ouseburn Arches Car Park on Stepney Bank | **Hours** Thu – Sun 11am – 4pm | **Tip** The neighbouring Ouseburn Farm is another family-friendly attraction in the Ouseburn Valley. A working farm, children can learn about animal husbandry and caring for the natural world in a fun and supportive environment (Ouseburn Road, Newcastle, NE1 2PA, +44 (0)191 232 3698, www.ouseburnfarm.org.uk).

78 Shields Ferry

Connecting North and South Shields

Criss-crossing the Tyne day after day, the Shields Ferry is a vital transport link between the towns of North and South Shields. At this point along the Tyne, just a mile and a half from Tynemouth, the river is too wide for a bridge to be economical or even practicable to build. Today, the Shields Ferry is the only ferry service on the Tyne, but in the early 20th century there were 11 different ferry routes between Newburn and Tynemouth. This whittling down of routes is a fascinating reflection of the changes to Tyneside in the past 50 years.

There is compelling documentary evidence that people have been crossing the Tyne by ferry between North and South Shields since 1377. By 1588, the service was so well established that ferries were forbidden from carrying beggars from one side of the river to the other. In pre-industrial times, the ferries that crossed the Tyne were at the mercy of both the weather and the tides. When conditions were rough, the passage could be a hairy experience and occasionally lives were lost.

In 1828, the North Shields Ferry Company was awarded the charter to run the first regular steam-powered ferry service. The first boat of this new, improved service was the *Baron Newcastle*. She was replaced in 1830 by the *Durham* and the *Northumberland*. Unfortunately for passengers, both of these ferries had an alarming inclination to run aground. Despite this they both remained in service until 1883.

The use of ferries peaked in the 1920s, when they were used daily by thousands of workers heading for the river's various shipyards. Ferry services were even introduced to carry cars across the river as they became more common. It was, however, the decline of industry on Tyneside, and the opening of the Tyne Tunnel in 1967 that killed all but the Shields Ferry off. Now the river is a quieter place, but, it has to be said, a far, far safer one.

Address 7 Ferry Mews, North Shields NE29 6LG (North Shields ferry landing), Ferry Street, South Shields NE33 1JR (South Shields ferry landing), www.nexus.org.uk/ferry | **Getting there** Bus (North Shields) 19 to New Quay–Ferry, (South Shields) 10, E1 and T503 to Ferry Street–Coronation Street | **Hours** See website for schedule | **Tip** Arbeia in South Shields is a reconstructed Roman fort that vividly conveys how life was lived in a garrison at the edge of the Roman Empire (www.arbeiaromanfort.org.uk).

79 Side Gallery

Focusing on the north east

One of the few constants in life is continuous change. If you don't pay attention it's all too easy to forget how things once were. Thank goodness then for the documentary photographers and film-makers of Amber, who have been recording life in the north east since 1969. Amber now has an astonishing archive of images of the region from those five decades. The Side Gallery is the principal showcase for the group's endeavours, as well as a venue to celebrate the power of documentary photography more generally.

The most renowned member of Amber is the Finnish documentary photographer Sirkka-Liisa Konttinen. Konttinen moved to Byker in 1969, having studied photography in London. Over a period of seven years, Konttinen photographed her fellow residents of Byker. At the time, the town was undergoing radical change with the demolition of the old terraced housing and the building of the Byker Wall (see ch. 12). Konttinen continued to live and work in Byker until her own home there was demolished. The project led to the book *Byker*, which was published to great acclaim and described by the writer David Alan Mellor as bearing 'witness to her intimate embeddedness in the locality'.

Konttinen has continued to document northern life, including North Shields dance schools in *Step by Step*, and the effects of the coal industry in *Coal Coast*. In 2003, Konttinen returned to Byker to shoot *Byker Revisited*, which is an evocative look at how different Byker now is. In 2011, Konttinen's photos were added to the UNESCO Memory of the World register, and described as being 'of outstanding national value and importance to the United Kingdom'. With accolades like that it's fair to say that the north east is lucky to have Konttinen. Without her (and the other members of Amber) the region's collective memory would have more gaps. And there wouldn't be a thing we could do to change that.

Address 5–9 Side, Newcastle, NE1 3JE, +44 (0)191 232 2208, www.amber-online.com/side-gallery | **Getting there** Bus Q1/Q3 Quaylink to Quayside Guildhall | **Hours** Tue–Sun 11am–5pm | **Tip** The North East Art Collective is dedicated to supporting local artists and selling their work. The gallery displays all genres of artwork, including oils, watercolours and photography (45 Eldon Garden, Newcastle, NE1 7RA, +44 (0)191 231 2483, www.northeastartcollective.co.uk).

80__ Space Invaders

Aliens infiltrate Tyneside

In the paranoid 1950s, the human race was warned to keeping watching the skies. Greedy alien eyes were watching the Earth, eager to steal the planet from us. When the time was right they would strike and that would be that for humanity. Constant vigilance was our only hope of averting attack. And it worked. For a while. But now they are here, amongst us, and barely anyone has noticed...

Scattered across Newcastle and Gateshead, positioned high and unobtrusively above head height, are over 20 small but colourful ceramic mosaics based on characters from the 1980s *Space Invaders* arcade game. They were all installed in 2006 by a French artist known as 'Invader' to celebrate the *Spank the Monkey* exhibition at BALTIC (see ch. 6). 'Invader' has installed similar mosaics in other cities around the world, including Mombasa and São Paulo. Fortunately, these aliens have made no attempt at invasion. Yet.

Fittingly, the simplest to get close to – once you've climbed 203 stairs – is an invader hidden in the stairwell of the BALTIC. Others you can find south of the Tyne include three in Gateshead Interchange Metro Station, and one close to Sage Gateshead (see ch. 75). In Newcastle, you can spot an invader at the south end of Stowell Street, another high up on a column supporting Commercial Union House on Pilgrim Street, and one guarding the entrance to Eldon Lane. There are others, but half the fun is finding them for yourself. You can even see how many points in total your sightings are worth, using an online map.

Strangely, not all of the invaders date from 2006. Some even represent characters from other arcade games. Does this mean that 'Invader' has made more visits to the region? Has a copycat decided to follow in his footsteps? Or – more sinister still – is the threat mutating and entering a final and deadlier phase? Find them all before it truly is Game Over.

Address Invader's website: www.space-invaders.com; locations: www.heritageandhistory.com |
Tip That Retro Game Shop in the Grainger Market is a cornucopia of second-hand consoles,
controllers and computer games (Unit 145, Grainger Market, Newcastle, NE1 5QW).

81 Spanish City

The original pleasure dome?

The Edwardians knew a thing or two about creating stylish coastal resorts. They built piers, luxury hotels and, in Whitley Bay, a sparkling white pleasure palace called Spanish City.

Spanish City was built for Charles Elderton, a show-business entrepreneur. After the failure of a tour of the Isle of Man with a group of entertainers named The Toreadors, Elderton moved on to run the Theatre Royal in Hebburn. There he created a new group of Toreadors, who performed in Whitley Park within an enclosure of Spanish street scenes painted on canvas awnings. A success, this led to the area being renamed Spanish City. Over a few short years, the range of entertainments quickly grew, including the addition of a fairground.

What was needed, though, was a more permanent structure. In February 1910 work began on the building seen today. Constructed using reinforced concrete, Spanish City took a mere 60 days to complete. Despite this speed, Spanish City's dome was once the biggest in the country after St Paul's Cathedral.

Over the course of the 20th century, the fortunes of Spanish City waxed and waned. It was used to house troops during World War I. Scuffed and a bit battered, it was restored during the 1920s, to become a popular ballroom. During World War II the dome was camouflaged with grey paint and a covering of netting, with soldiers billeted in the building once more.

Post-war, people again flocked to Whitley Bay to enjoy themselves, but this was not to last. Cheap foreign holidays gradually reduced visitor numbers. Threatened with demolition when the structure was deemed unsafe, Spanish City seemed doomed. For nearly 16 years the building was closed and only ultimately saved with a £10-million investment. In 2018, visitors said 'Hola' to the new Spanish City, a leisure venue with a choice of restaurants and cafés inside to suit every taste.

Address Spanish City, Spanish City Plaza, Whitley Bay, NE26 1BG, +44 (0)191 691 7090, www.spanishcity.co.uk | **Getting there** Bus 1A Coaster, 1B Coaster, 308 or 309 Cobalt and Coast to Whitley Bay Park Avenue; Metro to Whitley Bay (Yellow Line), then a 15-minute walk; paid parking at Spanish City Car Park | **Hours** Daily 9am–5pm | **Tip** Whitley Bay beach is a 2-mile expanse of golden sand, popular with locals and visitors alike. At the northern end is St Mary's Island, home to an iconic lighthouse.

82 Sparkie Williams

The talkative budgie who inspired an opera

In a cabinet in the Living Planet gallery of the Great North Museum: Hancock are the remains of Sparkie Williams, a small yellow and green budgerigar. He may look slightly out of place next to the more exotic animals on display nearby, but Sparkie was no ordinary bird.

Sparkie was hatched in 1954 in an aviary in Houghton-le-Spring. It was there that Mrs Mattie Williams saw and bought him. She called him Sparkie as he was 'a bright little spark'. Mattie first taught him to say 'Pretty Sparkie', before trying other phrases, such as her home address in case Sparkie escaped, as well as nursery rhymes and songs. By the time he was three and a half years old, Sparkie had a 500-word repertoire (spoken with a Geordie accent), and was ready for the big time.

In July 1958, Sparkie was entered into the BBC International Cage Bird Contest. He won so convincingly that Mattie was persuaded not to enter him again. Not that this mattered to Sparkie: he was now a star. He was contracted to Capern's bird seed for two years to head an advertising campaign; he appeared on the BBC's *Tonight* programme; and he was 'interviewed' by Philip Marsden, a renowned budgie expert. (The interview was later released by Parlophone as the B-side of a single, with *Sparkie the Fiddle* – a Raymond Chandler-esque short play – on the A-side.)

Sadly, Sparkie died in 1962. Touchingly, his last words were to tell Mattie that he loved her. Sparkie was preserved and donated to the Hancock, where he has been ever since. However, like any chatterbox, he could not be kept quiet. Inspired by the story, Michael Nyman and Carsten Nicolai created the opera *Sparkie: Cage and Beyond*. On 29 March, 2009, the opera was performed at the Haus der Berliner Festspiele in Berlin, to an enthusiastic audience. If he had been there, it is possible that Sparkie would have talked about nothing else for days afterwards.

Address Great North Museum: Hancock, Barras Bridge, Newcastle, NE2 4PT, +44 (0)191 208 6765, www.greatnorthmuseum.org.uk | **Getting there** Metro to Haymarket (Yellow or Green Line), then an 8-minute walk along B 1318 | **Hours** Mon–Fri 10am–5pm, Sat 10am–4pm, Sun 11am–4pm | **Tip** An entire gallery of the Great North Museum is devoted to Roman life in northern Britain, including a recreation of the route of Hadrian's Wall that stretches almost the length of the gallery.

83 Spirit of Jarrow
Onwards to London

Outside a busy supermarket in Jarrow is a poignant reminder of a significant event in the history of the town. *The Spirit of Jarrow* is a bronze sculpture by Graham Ibbeson, unveiled in 2001 to commemorate the 65th anniversary of the Jarrow Crusade. The work features two marchers holding a banner aloft, two children, a woman cradling a baby in her arms, and Paddy, a stray dog who became the Crusade's mascot. The group are walking out from the ribs of a ship, representing the root cause of the Crusade.

The north east did not have a good 1930s. The Great Depression saw a steep decline in manufacturing across the region, with a resulting loss of jobs. Jarrow, which relied heavily on shipbuilding, was particularly badly hit. In July 1936, David Riley, chairman of Jarrow Borough Council, gave a speech at a rally of unemployed men calling for a march on London, so that the 'government would then be forced to listen, or turn the military on us'. The idea of a protest march was adopted by other civic and political leaders in the town. Once the march reached London, a petition would be handed in to the Houses of Commons by Ellen Wilkinson, MP for Jarrow. The petition, eventually signed by over 11,000 people, demanded that the government '…should realise the urgent need that work should be provided for the town without further delay'.

On 5 October, 1936, 200 unemployed men set out for the capital. For 26 days, the men walked south, averaging 13 miles per day. They were generally welcomed in every town in which they spent the night, with many acts of touching kindness helping them on their way. On 4 November, Wilkinson handed in the petition as planned. Ultimately, the Crusade achieved little, with the town's pleas largely ignored by an indifferent government. Despite this, the men deserve to be remembered: their fight for a better life for all is still relevant today.

Address Viking Precinct, Jarrow, NE32 3LP | Getting there Bus 5, 9, 10, 11 or 26 Crusader to Cambrian Street–Morrisons; Metro to Jarrow (Yellow Line), then a 7-minute walk; free parking at nearby shopping centre | Tip Campbell Park is a large green space south of Jarrow where you can visit Bede's Well, an Edwardian folly built in 1908 dedicated to the Venerable Bede, who was born in nearby Monkton (Monkton Lane, Jarrow, NE31 2XQ).

84__Sports Day
Quirky sculpture shows we can all win

Sport is important to Gateshead for a number of reasons. The Gateshead Stadium is a nationally renowned athletics venue, for instance. And then there's the Great North Run, a half marathon from Newcastle to South Shields, held annually since 1981. Seeing thousands of happy runners cross the Tyne Bridge into and through Gateshead should make anyone from the town feel justifiably proud.

That first Great North Run was the idea of (now Sir) Brendan Foster, a 10,000 metre bronze medalist at the 1976 Olympics in Montreal. Foster, who was born in Hebburn, was inspired by seeing the Round the Bays fun run in New Zealand. On 28 June, 1981, 12,000 people took part in the inaugural Great North Run – a relatively small number now, but an astonishing result at the time.

Since 1981, numerous records have been broken. In 2011, it was the race itself that was the record breaker when 54,000 people took part, making it the biggest half marathon in the world – taking the honour from the Gothenburg Half Marathon. Coincidentally, 2011 also saw the course record broken when the Kenyan Martin Mathathi finished in a mind-boggling time of 58:56 (or 2.25 miles every ten minutes!). In 2014, Tracey Cramond became the millionth participant to complete the run. But the oddest achievement has to be that of Tony 'The Fridge' Morrison, who regularly runs carrying an 88lb fridge on his back to raise money for charity.

But what about people who lack the drive or even the ability to take part in the run? Gateshead's *Sports Day* sculpture by Mike Winstone in Gateshead is a quirky take on sporting achievement. The main figure, with a jaunty spiked haircut, is obviously participating in a sack race. However, he is not alone. The presence of a tortoise and hare are a reminder that it's not always the swiftest who wins a race. A consolation to both runners and armchair athletes alike. Though a 13-mile sack race does not bear thinking about…

Address West Street, Gateshead, NE8 1DD | Getting there Bus 1A Coaster, 25, 27 Crusader, 28, 56 Fab or 57 CityLink and various others to Gateshead Interchange; Metro to Gateshead (Yellow or Green Line); paid parking at Charles Street Short Stay Car Park | Tip Nearby Trinity Square Gateshead is a new shopping and leisure centre, with a wide range of shops and restaurants, as well as a multi-screen cinema.

85 St Andrew's Churchyard

The company you keep

St Andrew's Church in Newcastle is the oldest in the city, with parts dating back to the 12th century. Thanks to its longevity it also has some of the most interesting graves in the city too. One of the earliest graves is that of Sir Aymer de Atholl who died in 1402, and his wife, the Lady Mary. A Sheriff of Northumberland, de Atholl donated the land now known as the Town Moor to the Freemen of Newcastle (see ch. 94).

Possibly the most distinguished of St Andrew's guests is Charles Avison, who was a major English 18th-century concerto composer and music essayist. His music is in the Baroque style, and includes compositions for the harpsichord and string quartet. The music historian Charles Burney described Avison after his death in 1770 as 'an ingenious and polished man, esteemed and respected by all that knew him'. Avison has a wonderfully descriptive gravestone in the churchyard, below which he spends eternity with his wife, son and grandson.

Less fortunate was the artist Luke Clennell, who died in 1840. Clennell is seen as one of the most talented pupils of Northumbrian artist Thomas Bewick. He suffered a nervous breakdown when his young wife died in 1817, which ultimately led to admission to Newcastle's lunatic asylum on Bath Lane, where he spent most of the rest of his life until his death in 1840. The location of Clennell's remains is a mystery as he was interred in an unmarked grave. His short, tragic life is commemorated by a marble tablet decorated with a painters' palette, added by friends to the church's chancel wall.

Hemmed in on all sides, space is limited in the churchyard. There have been no burials there since 1939, with one touching exception. During work on the church in 2010 several graves were disturbed. The remains of those for whom records were missing were reinterred together as people whose 'names and service are known only to God'.

Address Newgate Street, Newcastle, NE1 5SS, +44 (0)191 232 7935, www.standrewsnewcastle.org.uk | Getting there Bus 12, 12A, 21 Angel or Q3 QuayCity to Newcastle Newgate Street; Metro to Monument (Yellow or Green Line); paid parking at The Gate Car Park | Tip Cherryburn, the birthplace of Thomas Bewick, is now in the hands of the National Trust. The family's cottage is open to visitors. Here you can see a fascinating exhibition about Bewick and his work (Station Bank, Stocksfield, Northumberland, NE43 7DD).

86 St George's Church
Art and crafts

A local landmark, the 154-foot-high campanile of St George's Church in Jesmond was inspired by St Mark's in Venice. However – stylish though it is – the campanile isn't the true glory of the church; to see that you have to go inside. For a relatively small building, the interior is impressively lofty and feels more like a cathedral than a parish church.

St George's was designed by Thomas Ralph Spence and consecrated by Ernest Wilberforce – the first Bishop of Newcastle – in 1888. The money to build St George's was provided by Charles Mitchell, a parishioner and a business partner of Lord Armstrong. Mitchell's wealth enabled him to hire skilled craftsmen and artists, and to specify that only the finest materials be used. The result is a visual feast. The architecture historian Sir Nikolaus Pevsner thought highly of St George's, praising its 'expensive and tasteful decoration, very progressive in style for its date…'. Stylistically, the fixtures and fittings – intricately floral – belong to the Arts and Crafts movement.

The huge and elaborate wooden pulpit was carved by local artist Ralph Hedley. Hedley also created the Bishop's throne for St Nicholas' when Newcastle was granted city status in 1882. He also worked with Joseph Swan, producing moulds for Swan's experiments with light bulbs (see ch. 57). It is thought that Hedley suggested a pear shape for Swan's light bulb, a design still familiar today.

The local firm of Emley and Sons was responsible for the high altar, which was carved out of a solid piece of variegated pavonazzo marble. Surrounding the altar are Byzantine-influenced mosaics, depicting Christian symbols. The lower mosaics were all created *in situ*, with each tile placed by hand. There is so much detail that repeated visits are a must. Each time you'll discover something new, which is a fitting testament to Mitchell and Spence's vision.

Address St George's Close, Jesmond, NE2 2TF, +44 (0)191 281 1659, www.stgeorgesjesmond.org.uk | **Getting there** Bus 33 or 33A to Osborne Road–Lindisfarne Road; Metro to West Jesmond (Yellow or Green Line), then a 10-minute walk, limited on-street parking nearby | **Tip** Jam Jar on Osborne Road is a cool café-bar offering a menu that leans heavily into comfort food territory, with a wide range of tempting drink options (88 Osborne Road, Jesmond, NE2 2AP, +44 (0)191 281 4224, www.jamjarjesmond.co.uk).

87 St James' Park

Howay the Toon

There's a good argument to be made that St James' Park is the true centre of Newcastle. Home of Newcastle United, it is the focus of the city's hopes and dreams whenever the team play at home. St James' has been a football ground since 1880, though of course much enlarged and updated since then. The current stadium can hold over 52,000 people. Remarkably, the average attendance is never far below this figure.

Despite being only the eighth largest stadium in England, St James' does punch above its weight. It is, after all, home to the largest supporters' flag in European football. And, in 2018, it came first in a poll by fan website Football Ground Map to rate the atmosphere of Premier League stadiums.

St James' Park has four stands: the Gallowgate End, the East Stand, the Leazes End and the Milburn Stand. The Gallowgate End is named after the route taken by condemned prisoners from Newgate Gaol to the city gallows. The gallows stood on the Town Moor and were last used in 1844. On one particularly grim day in 1650, 22 people were hanged there. The Milburn Stand is named after Jackie Milburn, one of Newcastle United's star players in the 1950s. Born in Ashington, Milburn was the club's top goal scorer until his record was broken by Alan Shearer in 2006.

Perhaps the oddest thing about the stadium is the disagreement about its name. Is it St James' or St James? Officially it is St James', which is the name used by the club. However, the local Metro station does without the apostrophe. To add to the confusion, should the name be pronounced with one 's' or two? What isn't disputed is the anger of fans when the owner of the club, Mike Ashley, renamed St James' Park the Sports Direct Arena in November 2011. Although no one used the new name – except possible Ashley himself – there was rejoicing when it officially reverted to St James' Park less than a year later.

Address Strawberry Place, Newcastle, NE1 4ST, +44 (0)344 372 1892, www.nufc.co.uk | Getting there Bus 12, 39, 40, 62, 63 or 71 and various others to Barrack Road – St James Park; Metro to St James (Yellow Line); paid parking at St James Metro Car Park | Hours Usually viewable from outside only, except on match days. Those with a head for heights can take a rooftop tour to view the pitch from a height of 150 feet | Tip The Earl of Pitt Street pub has a self-described 'Alfred Hitchcock meets Vivienne Westwood' vibe. Food from an à la carte menu is served Thu–Sun (70 Pitt Street, Newcastle, NE4 5ST, +44 (0)191 261 7744, www.earlofpittstreet.co.uk).

88 Stottie Cake

Better than sliced bread

It's a poor reflection on a region or city if it doesn't have at least one local delicacy it can call its own. Cornwall has its pasties, Cheddar its cheese, and London – for some unaccountable reason – has made jellied eels a culinary speciality. The north east can lay claim to kippers (or can it? See ch. 40), Singin' Hinnies, Pan Haggerty, Floddies, and – perhaps the finest foodstuff of them all – the stottie cake, or just stottie if you're in a hurry.

The stottie is a bread, round and flat in shape, and with a heavy and satisfyingly chewy texture. The origin of the name is a mystery, but possibly derives from stot – Geordie for bounce – as a proper stottie should bounce when dropped, rather than limply plop and fall apart. The phrase 'stotting down with rain' – another useful Geordie phrase – refers to rain that falls so hard that it, too, bounces.

Stotties have been eaten by the rich and famous. Muhammad Ali was pictured tucking into one on a visit to the region in 1977 (see ch. 2). Queen Elizabeth II was gifted one on a royal trip to the north east, but was apparently slightly perplexed when told it was bread (whether the stottie later received the royal seal of approval has never made the public domain).

There are no exotic ingredients in a stottie: just flour, seasoning, milk or water and yeast. The latter ingredient is possibly the most surprising, as the stottie does look more like unleavened bread than a traditional loaf. The secret? Stottie is only allowed to 'prove' once, rather than twice like 'normal' bread. Proving is when bread is allowed to sit before baking to allow yeast to work its magic. The best place in Newcastle to buy stottie to make your own sandwich is Pink Lane Bakery. What you do with yours is a personal matter, but the connoisseur of the stottie cake fills it with ham and pease pudding. Just be careful not to drop it as you tuck in.

Recipes for stottie cake can be easily found on the Internet too.

Address Pink Lane Bakery, 40 Pink Lane, Newcastle, NE1 5DY, +44 (0)191 261 0606, www.pinklanebakery.co.uk | **Getting there** Bus 10, 11 or 38 to Central Station Neville Street; Metro to Central Station (Yellow or Green Line); paid parking at Newcastle Station Car Park | **Hours** Mon–Sat 8am–4pm | **Tip** The nearby Forth Hotel is a pub and eatery with an appealing mix of the contemporary and traditional, with a roof terrace for those hardy enough to drink outside – coat optional (Pink Lane, Newcastle, NE1 5DW, www.theforthnewcastle.co.uk).

89_ The Strawberry

Have a pre-match pint

It's thirsty work being a football fan. Shouting on the terraces for 90 minutes can leave a throat in serious need of lubrication. For fans of Newcastle United there's only one place to sink a pint and that's in The Strawberry, just two minutes' walk from the Gallowgate end of St James' Park. Inside you can find pictures and memorabilia celebrating the history of the Toon all the way up to the present day.

What isn't immediately obvious is why a pub so close to a football stadium should be named after a soft summer fruit, one associated more with tennis than the Beautiful Game.

In the 1700s there was no St James' Park and football was more like a semi-organised riot than the game played today. The story goes that the grounds near the Gallowgate belonged to the nuns of St Bartholomew's on Newgate Street. They used the land to cultivate strawberries, which were used to make strawberry wine. The wine was then sold despite threats of excommunication by the Bishop of Durham. The nuns continued to flout the Bishop's wishes until 1840 when the nunnery finally closed. Or did they? It's a great tale but one that runs into the problem of King Henry VIII. In 1540, the monarch had St Bartholomew's nunnery closed and the land sold to Newcastle Corporation.

What isn't in doubt is that in his will of 1859, John Brunton left '…all that tenement or dwelling house, the lower part whereof to be used as a beer house'. The Strawberry was officially up and running. At first the pub largely served people who were visiting nearby pleasure gardens. However, change was coming. St James' Park was built in 1880 and then, in 1930, a 4,000-capacity boxing hall was built nearby. Demolished when St James Metro was built, the hall hosted fights with greats like Sonny Liston. Through all these alterations The Strawberry has remained a constant. Which really *is* something to shout about.

Address 7–8 Strawberry Place, Newcastle, NE1 4SF, +44 (0)191 232 6865, www.thestrawberrypub.co.uk | Getting there Bus 62, 63, 71, 72, 87 to Newcastle St James (Stand F) or 12, 39, 40, 84, 941 to Newcastle St James (Stand E); Metro to St James (Yellow Line); paid parking at St James Metro Car Park | Hours Mon–Sat 11am–11pm, Sun 11am–10.30pm | Tip Newcastle United FC Sportswear Shop sells everything a Newcastle United fan could possibly want, from the latest strip to souvenirs and signed memorabilia (St James' Park, Strawberry Place, Newcastle, NE1 4ST, www.nufcdirect.com).

90_Swing Bridge

Spin me right round, baby

For nearly 2,000 years, people have been crossing the Tyne roughly where the Swing Bridge now straddles the river. The first bridge was built by the Romans, to serve a settlement known as Pons Aelius (or Aelian Bridge). A second, built in the 13th century, was both a crossing and a street of shops and houses. This bridge, along with many others along the Tyne, was swept away by the Great Flood of 1771. An elegant replacement was completed in 1781, but this bridge was fated to last a mere 87 years.

The problem was simple: the low arches of the bridge prevented shipping from sailing upriver. One man particularly affected was William Armstrong, who required a navigable route to the North Sea for his engineering works at Elswick. In 1850, the Tyne Improvement Commission was formed to stimulate trade along the river. The result was that the Georgian bridge was demolished in 1868 and work began on the Swing Bridge, which opened in 1876.

The secret to the Swing Bridge's success is that it can pivot through 360° on its axis, so allowing ships to pass by on either side. Two hydraulic engines – designed and built by Armstrong – are used to move the road platform. So well engineered are the engines that they are still in use today, though the Victorian steam pumps that originally drove them were replaced by electric pumps in 1959. The Swing Bridge immediately stimulated trade along the Tyne and opened frequently to river traffic; in the peak year of 1924 it swung open over 6,000 times. Due to the decline in industry, the bridge opens far less frequently now, mainly for pleasure boats rather than freight haulage.

One odd aspect of the bridge is that it is painted red and white, the colours of Sunderland FC, Newcastle's local football rivals. These colours help to prevent the metal of the bridge expanding on hot days, which could stop the bridge from opening.

Address Bridge Street, Newcastle, +44 (0)191 455 2671, www.portoftyne.co.uk | **Getting there** Bus Q2 Quaylink to Hillgate Quay; a 2-minute walk from the Close Swing Bridge Car Park | **Hours** During the annual Heritage Open Days festival, normally hidden areas of Newcastle, including the pump room of the Swing Bridge, are opened to the public. Tickets are generally on a first-come-first-served basis from www.heritageopendays.org.uk | **Tip** The Swing Bridge is just a 3-minute walk to The Cooperage, a 15th-century timber-framed building and one of the few quayside buildings to survive the Great Fire of 1854.

91 Talmudical College
A mini diaspora

If you want to study the Torah in Britain, then Gateshead is the place you need to be. The town has the country's fastest-growing strictly Orthodox Jewish community, largely centred around the neighbourhood of Bensham. Fittingly then, the Gateshead Talmudical College or *yeshiva* is the largest in Europe, and arguably the most significant outside Israel and the USA. The *yeshiva* has been described as the 'Oxbridge of the UK Jewish community', and teaches 350 male students from the north east, as well as a good number from Europe, North America and Africa.

The Jewish community in Gateshead is relatively recent. It all began in the 1780s when Jews fled from persecution in Russia to settle in Britain. The north east was a favoured destination due to direct shipping routes between the region's ports and those in the Baltic. By the late 19th century there was a sizeable Jewish community in Newcastle. In 1881, Zachariah Bernstone and – more importantly – Eliezer Adler crossed the Tyne to found a new community (or *kehillah*) in Gateshead, following their discontent with what they believed were the lax standards and anglicised character of Judaism in the city. Testifying to his role in helping to establish the *kehillah* in Gateshead, Adler's seat in the town's synagogue remains vacant to this day. The community grew slowly at first, though numbers swelled during the Nazi regime in Germany when European Jews again fled to Britain. Numbers have increased more rapidly in the 2000s largely due to the success of the *yeshiva*.

The *yeshiva* was founded in 1929 on Bewick Street, just five minutes' walk from the current building. The new *yeshiva* was built in 1961 to create space for a *beth hamedrash* or room used for prayer and study. The *yeshiva* has developed in the intervening years, including the building of Sebba House, a dormitory for 70 of the *yeshiva's* students.

Address 88 Windermere Street West, Gateshead, NE8 1UB | Getting there 54 Voltra, 866, S 844 or S 856 to Coatsworth Road – Grasmere Street; Metro Gateshead (Yellow or Green Line), then a 17-minute walk; on-street parking nearby | Hours Viewable from the outside only | Tip Gateshead Central Library is a handsome public building that offers a wide selection of books, the largest audiovisual library in the north east, and Bewick Café with its extensive menu of hot and cold food (Prince Consort Road, Gateshead, NE8 4LN, +44 (0)191 433 8410).

92 Theatre Royal

Don't mention The Scottish Play

There has been a Theatre Royal in Newcastle since 1788, when a Royal licence was granted by King George III. Originally the theatre stood on Drury Lane, but in 1837 it moved into a new building designed by John and Benjamin Green, its current home. For 62 years the theatre flourished. And then disaster struck.

On 23 November, 1899, Frank Benson and his company performed Shakespeare's play *Macbeth*. Uttering Macbeth in a theatre – other than during a performance – is considered unlucky, and so actors refer to it as The Scottish Play. If someone is foolish enough to accidentally blurt out the name they must immediately leave the theatre, spin round three times, spit, curse and knock (presumably sheepishly) on the theatre door to be let back in.

Someone in Benson's company must have slipped up, for early on the morning of 24 November smoke was seen coming from the theatre. Fire engines were called and the crews discovered that the stage was alight. The fire quickly spread, completely destroying the interior but miraculously leaving the stone exterior intact.

Enter theatre architect Frank Matcham, who was tasked with the job of restoration. The auditorium was rebuilt in a French Renaissance style, a confection of white, crimson and gold. The theatre was enlarged too, after land on either side was bought for the purpose. Astonishingly, it took only two years to go from burnt-out shell to a new theatre. When the first production – *The Forty Thieves* – was performed on 31 December, 1901, it must have felt as if an old friend had come back to life.

The auditorium was refurbished in the late 1980s, but in 2011 the theatre was temporarily closed to restore the interior to the original Matcham design, with authentic carpet sourced and wallpaper reprinted and hung. The theatre now sparkles again, ready to face the 21st century and further performances of *Ma…* The Scottish Play.

Address 100 Grey Street, Newcastle, NE1 6BR, +44 (0)8448 112 121 (Box Office),
www.theatreroyal.co.uk | Getting there Bus 1, 22, 22X, 54 Voltra and various others to
Monument Market Street; Metro to Monument (Yellow or Green Line) | Tip Harry's Bar
and Restaurant opposite the Theatre Royal is ideally placed for a pre-show meal or drink
(77 Grey Street, Newcastle, NE1 6EF, +44 (0)191 261 2621, www.harrysbarnewcastle.com).

93 Town Hall Clock

Little Ben

The Queen Elizabeth Tower – Big Ben – has a diminutive rival in Gateshead. Standing outside the old town hall, the north east's clock tower was made by Gillett & Johnston and erected in 1892. Painted a splendidly rakish black and gold, it's far smaller than the timepiece in London, but it is arguably just as handsome. It was presented to Gateshead by the then mayor, Walter de Lancey Willson, who was serving his second term, and who would go on to be mayor for a third time in 1902.

Willson founded the much-missed eponymous grocery store chain of Walter Willson's in 1875, dropping de Lancey from the name for entirely understandable reasons. Willson's first store on Newgate Street in Bishop Auckland was soon followed by other stores in villages and towns across County Durham, Northumberland and Cumbria (or Cumberland and Westmorland as they were then).

Willson moved the headquarters of his rapidly growing empire of 'smiling service stores' to Gateshead in 1887. By the time he died in 1907, he owned 104 shops and with the proceeds had bought himself a country retreat at Kirklinton Park, Cumbria. The running of the Walter Willson stores then fell to Stephen Aitchison, who had married Willson's eldest daughter Alice, and who had started out as a shop assistant in the original store. Stephen was knighted in 1928, then given a baronetcy in 1938. The family continued to acquire property, with Aitchison buying the ruined Lemmington Hall, Northumberland in 1916, to have it restored as a country home. The couple's son, Sir Walter de Lancey Aitchison bought Coupland Castle in 1938, lending Lemmington to the Convent of the Sacred Heart. Walter Willson's continued to be family-owned, though the number of stores slowly declined. In 1998, the remaining 48 stores were bought out by Alldays and re-named. And so, time was finally called on the Walter Willson brand.

Address West Street, Gateshead, NE8 1HE | Getting there Bus 1A Coaster, 25, 27 Crusader, 28, 56 Cityrider, 57 CityLink and various others to Gateshead Interchange; Metro to Gateshead (Yellow or Green Line); paid parking at Swinburne Street Car Park | Tip The Central is a pub just a few minutes' walk from the Old Town Hall. Known as 'The Coffin', its unusual wedge shape is due to its location below an intersection of three railway lines (Half Moon Lane, Gateshead, NE8 2AN, +44 (0)191 478 2543).

94　Town Moor Cows

Welcome to Moocastle

Newcastle is one of only two cities in the country that has a large open space at its centre where cattle can be grazed (Cambridge being the other). The space, known as the Town Moor, is roughly 400 hectares, making it larger than New York's Central Park or the combined size of London's Hyde Park and Hampstead Heath. The moor is open all year round for leisure, but it is only between April and October that the cattle come to stay. At the end of the season the cattle are moved on, either to market or for breeding. However, do not think of taking your own cow to the moor in order to feed it. This right is granted only to the Freemen of Newcastle.

Newcastle's Freemen were originally merchants and craftsmen who were members of companies (or guilds) that traded within the city's boundaries. Today, the Freemen title (which includes both men and women) is either inherited or conferred as an honorific.

Once the son or daughter of a Hereditary Freeman reaches 20, he or she is entitled to be sworn in as a Freeman by the Lord Mayor of Newcastle. One of the duties of a Hereditary Freeman is a readiness to defend the city from attack when called upon – less likely now than a few centuries ago. Honorary Freemen, such as President Jimmy Carter and footballer Alan Shearer, have the title conferred on them by Newcastle City Council, though the title cannot be passed on.

It is a rare Freeman who exercises their right to graze cattle; the right is usually sublet to local farmers. The Town Moor Act 1988 states that there should never be more than 800 cows on the moor at any one time, though the number seldom exceeds 600. The cattle are not allowed to calf on the moor either. Farmers who allow this to happen, even if accidentally, are charged. The cattle, placid creatures usually, rarely charge, though dogs out for a walk on the moor must be kept on a lead just in case.

Address Great North Road, Newcastle, NE2 4AN | Getting there Bus Q3 QuayCity, 30, 31 or 35 Great North Road–Forsyth Road | Tip During the last week of June, Newcastle's Town Moor is also home to The Hoppings, the biggest travelling fun fair in Europe with over 300 fairground attractions to choose from. The first Hoppings took place in 1882 and was a temperance event, organised with the aim of tempting people away from the (usually drink-fuelled) Race Week at Newcastle Racecourse.

95__Town Wall Towers

Fixer-uppers

Recycling isn't a modern concept; people have been sensibly reusing discarded things for millennia. Nowhere is this more apparent than the fate of three of Newcastle's surviving town wall towers, each of which has been put to other uses.

You can find the Morden Tower on the West Wall (see ch. 106). Its happy destiny was to become a literary venue after Tom and Connie Pickard had the idea of hosting poetry readings there. On 16 June, 1964, Pete Brown gave the first reading in the tower. The success of this event led to other poets being invited, including Ted Hughes, Seamus Heaney and American beat poet Allen Ginsberg. In 1965, local poet Basil Bunting was persuaded to read his epic work *Briggflatts* for the first time, to an enthusiastic response.

The Plummer Tower on Croft Street would now be unrecognisable to its original builders. After the need for a defensive wall receded, it was used as a meeting hall by the Company of Cutlers. In 1749, the lease to the tower was granted to the Company of Masons, who then proceeded to modify it. An upper storey and external staircase were added, as well as a Palladian frontage, which has a charming symmetry common to the style. Now the Plummer Tower is used as office space, and has Scheduled Ancient Monument status that prevents any further tinkering with its structure.

Overlooking the Tyne, the Sallyport Tower has had an equally dramatic facelift. After falling into disuse, it was leased to the Company of Shipwrights, who remodelled the building, adding the four decorative corner turrets that can be seen today. The name of the tower is thought to refer to the postern gate on the ground floor. It was from this gate that troops sallied forth during the Civil War to attack the Scots who besieged Newcastle in 1644. Spookily, there have been reports of a ghost haunting the tower, thought to be a defender killed during the siege.

Address Sallyport Tower, Tower Street, Newcastle, NE1 2HY | **Getting there** Bus Q3 QuayCity to City Road-Melbourne Street; Metro to Manors (Yellow Line), then a 5-minute walk; paid parking at Quayside Multi Storey Car Park | **Hours** Viewable from the outside only | **Tip** Live Theatre is dedicated to nurturing new writing talent, producing and presenting new plays, many of which win awards and transfer to London's West End (Broad Chare, Quayside, Newcastle, NE1 3DQ, www.live.org.uk).

96__Turbinia
Speeding across the ocean waves

Housed in an old Co-operative Wholesale Society building, the Discovery Museum is a showcase for Newcastle's rich industrial and social heritage. The largest exhibit by far – dominating the museum's central hall – is *Turbinia*, a 104-foot-long steamship. Built on Tyneside, *Turbinia* was cutting edge technology when launched in 1894. She was constructed at the instigation of Charles Parsons, who had recently invented a revolutionary new power plant.

Parsons was a superb engineer who came to Newcastle in 1877 as an apprentice at W. G. Armstrong, having read mathematics at Trinity College Dublin, and gained a first-class honours degree from St John's College, Cambridge. In 1884, Parsons created the world's first steam turbine. It was initially used to drive a dynamo – also developed by Parsons – to produce cheap electricity efficiently; a breakthrough that – happily for us – made the modern world possible. Parsons knew that his turbine also had the potential to make obsolete the steam engines then used in shipping. In 1893, Parsons set up the Parsons Marine Steam Turbine Company to further develop and manufacture his turbines. Now all he needed was a test vessel in which to install one of his steam turbines and prove their worth. And so, *Turbinia*.

After a few hiccups, *Turbinia*'s performance during trials justified Parsons' faith. She was known as his '…winning North Sea greyhound' after reaching a speed of 34 knots (roughly 39mph). Her winning potential was amply demonstrated in 1897, when she arrived unannounced at Spithead during a Navy Review for Queen Victoria's Diamond Jubilee. In front of the gathered crowd, *Turbinia* comfortably outran two lines of navy ships and a picket boat sent out to stop her. Parsons' steam turbine quickly became *the* way to power ships – notably in the Blue Riband-winning RMS *Mauretania* of 1906, fittingly also built on the Tyne.

Address Blandford Square, Newcastle, NE1 4JA, +44 (0)191 232 6789, www.discoverymuseum.org.uk | Getting there Bus 1, 30 or 31 to Westmorland Road–Discovery Museum; Metro to Central Station, then a 7-minute walk; paid parking at Blandford Square Public Car Park | Hours Mon–Fri 10am–4pm, Sat & Sun 11am–4pm, closed bank holidays | Tip The neighbouring Alphabetti Theatre features performances from emerging artists in the fields of music, theatre and comedy (St James' Boulevard, Newcastle, NE1 4HP, +44 (0)191 261 9125, www.alphabettitheatre.co.uk).

97_ Tyne Bridge

You know you're home when…

Step aside Angel of the North. If you ask someone to name an iconic symbol of the north east they will likely choose the Tyne Bridge. Spanning the Tyne at a height of 85 feet above the river, it is an engineering marvel. Started in August 1925, the bridge took three years to build, and consumed 7,112 tonnes of steel and over 770,000 rivets. The 1920s were not a time for health and safety regulations. The bridge builders worked high above the Tyne, without using ropes or any form of safety harness. Remarkably, however, only one person, a 33-year-old scaffold erector named Nathaniel Collins, died during the bridge's construction.

One persistent myth about the Tyne Bridge is that it was built as a dry-run for the design of the similar (but larger) Sydney Harbour Bridge in Australia. In fact, the Sydney Bridge was started earlier but, being a far bigger and more involved project, was completed three years after the Tyne Bridge. (Not that the Sydney Harbour Bridge was itself unique, as it more than resembles the Hell Gate Bridge in New York, opened in 1916.)

The Tyne Bridge was officially opened on 10 October, 1928, by King George V, who, with Queen Mary, was the first to cross in a vehicle, a horse-drawn Ascot landau. Since then, the bridge has been the main road link between Newcastle and Gateshead. Now, over 70,000 cars cross the bridge daily, with sitting in a peak-time traffic jam a rite of passage for any Geordie who has recently passed their driving test. This heavy usage means that the bridge needs regular maintenance. The distinctive green paint used to protect the steel structure – BS14C39/Greenwood – has an 18-year lifespan. Between 2,200 to 3,300 gallons of paint is used every time a fresh coat is applied. To add to the stresses and strains on the structure, over 50,000 people annually run over the bridge on the first leg of the 13-mile Great North Run (see ch. 84).

Address Newcastle, NE1 3AE | **Getting there** Bus Q1 Quaylink to Hillgate | **Tip** Newcastle's Guildhall, near the Tyne Bridge, was once used as an administrative centre for the city. The classical Grade I-listed building is not open to the public except on organised tours. Highlights include the old courtroom, and local scenes painted by George Bouchier Richardson.

98__ Tyne Theatre

Take centre stage

The Victorians knew how to do theatres. The Tyne Theatre & Opera House is one of the finest in the country. A Grade I-listed building, it is rated by English Heritage as being in the top four per cent of listed buildings. That the theatre still exists is a minor miracle, however. Its history is one of initial success followed by waning fortunes, with the occasional disaster thrown in.

The Tyne Theatre opened in 1867 at the instigation of Joseph Cowen, a local businessman and MP. For 40 years the theatre thrived, but falling attendance during World War I saw the theatre close in 1917. In 1919, it reopened as The Stoll Picture Theatre to show movies, the first of which was *Tarzan of the Apes*. In 1932, The Stoll was the first cinema in Newcastle to show a 'Talkie'. Unfortunately, attendance had dropped by the 1960s, largely due to the advent of television (see ch. 101). To counter this, X-rated movies were shown. This failed to stop the decline and so, in 1974, after a showing of *Danish Bed and Board*, The Stoll closed.

In 1977, Jack Dixon discovered the abandoned theatre. With friends, he started the 'Save the Stoll' campaign. Through fundraising, and with the help of a small army of volunteers, Dixon did exactly that. After the foundation of a preservation trust, work began to restore the theatre ready for live performances once more. Remarkably, the original Victorian stage machinery was still in place, and is still used for productions today.

This machinery was almost lost in 1985 when a fire broke out backstage. The indefatigable Dixon led the rebuilding project. After extensive repair work costing £1.5 million, the theatre was open again within 11 months. Since 2015, the theatre has been an independent venue, managed by the Tyne Theatre & Opera House Ltd. Now profits from productions are used to maintain this remarkable building for future generations to enjoy.

Address 117 Westgate Road, Newcastle, NE1 4AG, +44 (0)191 243 1171, www.tynetheatreandoperahouse.uk | **Getting there** Bus 10, 11, 38, 38A, 71, 72 or 87 to Westgate Road–Rutherford Street; Metro to Central Station (Yellow or Green Line); paid parking at Blandford Square Public Car Park | **Tip** FLIP near the Tyne Theatre sells original vintage American clothing from classic tee-shirts to stylish stetsons (104 Westgate Road, Newcastle, NE1 4AF, +44 (0)191 233 1755, www.flipvintage.com).

99 Tynemouth Priory

Repeatedly picking up the pieces

The high cliffs of Pen Bal Crag overlooking the mouth of the Tyne are the ideal place to defend against invasion from the North Sea. The first to discover this were Anglo-Saxon monks, who built a priory there in the 8th century. Unfortunately, though their thinking was sound, the priory was repeatedly attacked by Vikings in the 800s. Sometimes the defenders succeeded in repelling the onslaught, but generally the Scandinavians had the upper hand. By 875 the priory buildings had largely been destroyed.

Gradually, once the threat of Viking invasion had receded, monks returned to Pen Bal Crag. By 1050 a church had been established on the headland. This was unfortunate timing. After the Norman invasion of 1066, William the Conqueror embarked on a brutal campaign to subjugate northern England, known as the 'Harrying of the North'. One consequence was the destruction of the church.

Stability finally came in 1090 when a new Tynemouth Priory was founded by Robert de Mowbray, created Earl of Northumberland by King William II. Under his protection, the Priory flourished. Mowbray also established a castle next to the Priory, a motte-and-bailey structure that eventually developed into a substantial stone fortification, the gatehouse of which is still standing today. This defensive capability helped the priory survive attacks by Robert the Bruce during Scottish raids south in the years following the Battle of Bannockburn in 1314.

Over the next several centuries, Tynemouth Priory became rich and powerful. This would not last, as the Priory came under attack for what would be the last time. This time the threat was not external. In 1533, King Henry VIII broke with Rome to create the Church of England, taking the opportunity to suppress the monasteries and plunder their land and wealth. Tynemouth Priory was finished, gradually falling into disrepair and destined not to be rebuilt.

Address Pier Road, Tynemouth, NE30 4BZ, +44 (0)191 257 1090, www.english-heritage.org.uk | Getting there Bus 306 to Tynemouth Village; free parking for two hours Priors Haven Car Park, paid parking at Spanish Battery Car Park | Hours Mon–Fri Apr–Sep 10am–6pm daily, Oct–Nov 10am–5pm daily, Nov–Mar 10am–4pm Sat & Sun (closed 24–26 Dec & 1 Jan) | Tip Gareth James Chocolatier is an independent artisan chocolatier on Tynemouth's Front Street. All of the mouth-watering confectionery is made on the premises.

100 — Tynemouth Station

The St Pancras of the North?

Since 1980, the Metro light rail system has smoothly moved people around Tyneside. The Metro was not created entirely from scratch, however. Although new stations were built to serve Newcastle's suburbs, many of the stations along the Metro's coastal stretch were originally created for the North Eastern Railway company in the 19th century.

The most striking of these older stations is Tynemouth Station. Built in 1882, it was designed by William Bell, NER's Chief Architect, and replaced an older station from 1847. The new station was necessary as, during the late-Victorian and early Edwardian periods, the resorts of Tynemouth, Cullercoats and Whitley Bay were increasingly popular with holidaymakers. To cope with the number of visitors, the platforms were built 656 feet in length, unusually long for a small town station.

The platforms are not the true glory of the station, however. For that you need to look upwards. Way above head height are glass canopies that give the station a spacious and airy feel. Supported by cast-iron columns and spandrels filled with decorative circular and diamond motifs, the canopies zig-zag in a ridge-and-furrow design for the entire length of the station. The survival of these canopies is entirely due to local campaigning. Over the 20th century, time and neglect took its toll on the roof; damaged sections of the glazing were often replaced by sheets of corrugated iron. Although the station was granted a Grade II* listing in 1978, it was in poor condition when British Rail handed it over to Tyneside Passenger Transport Authority. It was only in 1987, with the formation of the Friends of Tynemouth Station, that restoration began. The final phase of this work was completed in 2012, the 130th anniversary of the station's opening. Now the station feels as fresh and welcoming as Bell must have originally intended.

Address Tynemouth Station, Station Terrace, Tynemouth, NE30 4RE, www.nexus.org.uk/metro | **Getting there** Metro to Tynemouth Station (Yellow Line); paid parking on the west side of the station | **Tip** Every Saturday and Sunday from 9am–3.30pm the Friends of Tynemouth Station host a market in the grounds of the station. With over 150 stalls, you can find a wide range of things to buy from local suppliers (www.tynemouthmarkets.com).

101 Tyneside Cinema

Take a trip down memory lane

Astonishingly, in 1946 there were 1.64 billion cinema admissions in the UK. There was nowhere to go from there but downhill. In 1984, just 54 million admissions were recorded, a drop of almost 97 per cent. The culprit? Television, and then later the VCR and DVD player. Why go out when you could watch programmes in the comfort of your own home? With fewer ticket sales, many cinemas closed, the buildings either put to other uses or simply pulled down. This happened to a good number of cinemas in Newcastle: The Queens, The ABC, The Pavilion. All gone. Grandest of all was The Odeon, which entertained filmgoers for more than 70 years until its doors finally closed in 2002.

Hooray then for the Tyneside Cinema. Opened in 1937, it is the last surviving newsreel theatre in the country still in use as a cinema. The founder was Dixon Scott, great uncle to local film directors Sir Ridley and Tony Scott. Scott had grand plans for the Bijou News-Reel Cinema as it was then known. He wanted news to be available to all, and so newsreels were shown continuously throughout the day. This, Scott believed, would help people keep up with current events more easily – and cheaply – than by reading newspapers. And he wanted people to do this in stylish surroundings. And so Scott's cinema was decorated in the then-fashionable Art Deco style, with hints of the Middle and Far East added to the mix – inspired by his travels to those regions.

In celebration of the cinema's history, a specially selected archive newsreel is shown daily. Free to watch, these films from 1930s and 1940s show the news of the day, from both Tyneside and across the UK. However, the Tyneside Cinema is not stuck in the past. A major renovation project in 2008 restored the original auditorium, and added two new screens. Now the cinema can show art house films alongside the latest blockbusters. Good news for everyone.

Address 10 Pilgrim Street, Newcastle, NE1 6QG, +44 (0)191 227 5500, www.tynesidecinema.co.uk | Getting there Bus 1, 6, 30, 31, 33, 33A or 35 to Monument Pilgrim Street; Metro to Monument (Yellow or Green Line) | Hours Mon–Thu 8am–11pm, Fri & Sat 8am–midnight, Sun 10am–11pm | Tip Hoochie Coochie is an intimate bar and live music venue specialising in Funk, Soul and Jazz (54 Pilgrim Street, Newcastle, NE1 6SF, +44 (0)191 222 0130, www.hoochiecoochie.co.uk).

102_ Vampire Rabbit
Run away!

Rabbits. Harmless creatures you wouldn't normally cross the road to avoid. Admittedly, they do have large front teeth, but these are needed only to nibble their way through vegetation. Still, you cannot help but wonder what would happen should rabbits develop a taste for blood. Wonder no more: Newcastle has its very own carnivorous bunny, perched high above an ornate entranceway in an alley behind St Nicholas' Cathedral. The city's Vampire Rabbit looks down at all who pass, teeth bared and a hungry look in his eye.

Fortunately, the Vampire Rabbit is a stone carving, not a living (undead?) creature. It belongs to the Cathedral Buildings, a Jacobean-style confection of pink and white built in 1901. Why the rapacious rodent was added to the building is now a mystery, but there are a number of possibilities.

One theory is that he is not a rabbit at all but a hare, and is there as a tribute to Sir George Hare Philipson, a local doctor and friend of William Wood, one of the building's three architects. (Wood was a mason. Hares have masonic symbolism, so that is an option too.) The rabbit may also honour the engraver Thomas Bewick, who was famed for his animal studies and whose workshop once stood nearby. Arguably, though, Bewick, with his acute powers of observation, would not have drawn a rabbit with its ears on backwards, the way the Vampire Rabbit wears his.

These are the three most likely reasons. However, if you want a supernatural explanation, you only have to turn round to see a small car park directly in front of you. This covers what was once the cathedral's graveyard. The story goes that grave robbers were at their work one night when a rabbit mysteriously appeared and attacked them, draining them of their blood. If the rabbit is there to punish wrong-doers, then he is a good reason not to leave your car parked for a minute longer than the allotted time.

Address St Nicholas' Churchyard, Newcastle, NE1 1PF | Getting there Bus 1A/1B Coaster, 21 Angel, 27 Crusader, 56 Cityrider and 57 CityLink to High Level Bridge North End | Tip The cathedral is only a few minutes' walk away from the Bigg Market, a place for weekend drinking and clubbing and the reason for Newcastle's reputation as a party town.

103 Victoria Tunnel

Subterranean shortcut for coal

How do you get something efficiently from one place to another without inconveniencing anyone? Simple: you build a tunnel. This is precisely what Porter & Latimer, owners of Leazes Main Colliery, did. Built between 1839 and 1842, the Victoria Tunnel was used to transport coal along a waggonway from the colliery to the River Tyne. Opened with a cannon salute and a party for the workers, the tunnel was an immediate success. Unfortunately, the colliery it was built to serve closed just 18 years later. With rather less fanfare, the tunnel was closed and then largely forgotten about.

This changed in 1939 when war broke out and it was realised that the tunnel would make an excellent air raid shelter. At a cost of £37,000, seven new entrances were created and facilities – such as lighting and bunkbeds – added. Spending the night in the tunnel was not an appealing prospect; complaints that it was dark and damp were frequently made (though at least the coal dust had been cleaned out). As many realised, though, the tunnel was a safe place to be when bombs were raining down. Rather impertinently, a visiting civil servant claimed that '…as this is a mining district, the persons who will shelter in this tunnel are possibly better fitted constitutionally to resist underground and damp conditions than those in the South'.

The tunnel was abandoned again after VE Day. At the height of the Cold War the tunnel was almost converted into a nuclear fallout shelter, but this plan was dropped. Part of the tunnel had the indignity of being turned into a sewer in 1976, but otherwise it was out of sight and out of mind for the remainder of the 20th century. In 2006, Newcastle City Council was granted Heritage Lottery funding to restore a section of the tunnel and open it as a visitor attraction. Now the Ouseburn Trust run regular guided tours along a small stretch of the tunnel.

Address 55 Lime Street, Ouseburn Valley, Newcastle, NE1 2PQ, +44 (0)191 230 4210, www.ouseburntrust.org.uk | Getting there Bus 12, 39 or 40 to New Bridge Street – Blackfriars, then a 7-minute walk; Metro to Manors (Yellow Line), then a 14-minute walk; paid parking at the Ouseburn Arches Car Park on Stepney Bank | Tip Learn to ride a horse with qualified staff at the nearby Stepney Bank Stables (Stepney Bank, Newcastle, NE1 2NP, +44 (0)191 261 5544, www.stepneybank.co.uk).

104_ Volunteer Life Brigade

Keeping a watch since 1864

The North Sea can be a dangerous place. Thank goodness then for the Tynemouth Volunteer Life Brigade, ready and willing for over 150 years to help those in dire straits on these wild and restless waters. The fully trained volunteers are on call all year round, and work closely with HM Coastguard, the RNLI and other of the nation's emergency services.

It all started on the afternoon of 24 November, 1864, when a violent storm suddenly rumbled in from the south east. Out at sea were the schooner *Friendship* and the steamer *Stanley*, *en-route* to Aberdeen from London, carrying 30 passengers, 26 crew, and with cattle and sheep in pens on her open deck. With the weather worsening, both ships made for the shelter of the River Tyne.

The *Friendship* was the first of the pair to succumb to the gale, running ashore on Black Middens rocks close to the mouth of the Tyne. Due to the weather neither the North nor the South Shields lifeboats was able to get alongside the schooner, and so the rescue attempt was abandoned until the following day. All of the six crew were lost, including Daniel Page, the *Friendship*'s cabin boy. Then, at 5.30pm, with daylight fading, the *Stanley* foundered on the same rocks, colliding with the *Friendship*. Despite a valiant attempt at rescue, 26 more people died, two of whom were lifeboat crew.

On the 5 December, 1864, at a public meeting in North Shields, it was decided to form a voluntary service to help the Coastguard during emergencies. Over 100 men at the meeting signed up immediately, and so the Tynemouth Volunteer Life Brigade was formed.

The Brigade Watch House on the Spanish Battery is the home of the Brigade, where the volunteers train and where their rescue equipment is stored. A wonderful museum in the building tells the Brigade's story. From the South Tower you can also see across to Black Middens, where the story began all those years ago.

Address Brigade Watch House Museum, Spanish Battery, Tynemouth, NE30 4DD,
www.tvlb.org | Getting there Bus 306 to Tynemouth Village; Metro to Tynemouth (Yellow
Line), then a 14-minute walk; free parking for two hours Priors Haven Car Park, paid
parking at Spanish Battery Car Park | Hours Tue–Sat 10am–2.30pm, Sun 10am–noon |
Tip If you like the idea of the sea but don't want to get wet, then Tynemouth Aquarium is
the place for you. There you can see a wide variety of exotic fish from warmer waters, as
well as sea creatures native to the North Sea (Grand Parade, Tynemouth, NE30 4JF,
+44 (0)191 258 1031, www.tynemouthaquarium.co.uk).

105__Wallsend Metro Station

Finis muros

The clue is in the name. Wallsend is where Hadrian's Wall, a 73-mile-long boundary of stone and turf that marked the northern edge of the Roman Empire, came to an end (or began, depending on your viewpoint). North of the wall was unconquered territory. There lived wild men and women, belligerent, unwashed and lacking the social graces expected of Roman citizens.

To help keep the riff-raff out, the Romans built a fort at Wallsend which they named Segedunum. Roughly translated this means 'victory fort' or possibly 'strong fort'; it can't be denied that the Romans were masters of self-promotion. At its most populous, Segedunum housed two Roman cohorts, each cohort made up of 480 infantry and 120 cavalry. The fort was abandoned in the 5th century as the Roman Empire began to contract, before falling entirely.

In 1884, the remains of the fort were covered over when terraced housing was built for miners working at a nearby colliery. Segedunum was only uncovered again when the pit village was demolished in the 1970s. Now you can see the fort's excavated foundations by visiting Segedunum Roman Fort, run by Tyne and Wear Museums. Once there you can also wander round a recreated Roman bath house, or view the entire site from a 115-foot-high viewing platform above the visitors' centre.

You can drive to Segedunum but, if you want your funny bone tickled first, catching the Metro to Wallsend is by far the better option. The station is just III-minutes' walk from Segedunum, or 0.10587789473684185 Roman miles if you prefer. In 2003, to celebrate the town's Roman connection, Nexus, the operators of Tyne and Wear Metro, wittily updated the signs of Wallsend Metro Station. Instructions and directions can now be read in both English and Latin, the only railway station in the UK to offer this facility. Just make sure that you *gap sapiunt* as you step out onto the platform.

Platform 2
Suggestus II

No Smoking
Noli Fumare

Address Wooley Street, Wallsend, NE28 6HB | Getting there Bus 12, 41 Little Coasters, 40, 42, 42A, 553, Q3 QuayCity or 901 to Wallsend Metro; Metro to Wallsend (Yellow Line); free parking at Atkinson Terrace Car Park | Tip North of Wallsend, the Rising Sun Country Park is a 400-acre green space with a nature reserve and footpaths through grass and woodlands (Whitley Road, Benton, NE12 9SS).

106__ West Wall

Raise the gates, the Scots are coming...

England and Scotland have a long and often fractious joint history as neighbouring sovereign countries. During the medieval period, the two kingdoms jostled for supremacy in the border regions. This meant that invasion by Scotland was a constant nagging fear in the lives of Northumbrians, particularly in Newcastle, which was a rich and tempting plum. The solution was a 2-mile-long town wall, completed in the 14th century. At a height of 25 feet and 6 and a half feet thick, it was a forbidding show of strength.

To allow everyday movement in and out of the town, six fortified gates were built into the structure. These gates, all long gone, still live on in the names of streets or areas of Newcastle, such as Westgate, Newgate and Sandgate. As well as the gates, there were 17 towers, six of which have survived to the present, and a series of turrets with loopholes for archers. Between its construction and the 16th century, the wall proved a successful defence against the Scots. One of these failed attempts was led by William Wallace, later played by Mel Gibson in the film *Braveheart*. After his execution in London in 1305, parts of his body were put on display in Newcastle as a warning. It was only in 1644, during the War of the Three Kingdoms, that Scottish forces finally broke through the wall, staying in Newcastle until 1647.

Ultimately, it was peace not war that led to the destruction of the wall. After the 17th century, the threat of Scottish invasion receded and vanished altogether after the 1707 Acts of Union. The wall was then an impediment to the expansion of the city. From the 18th century onwards it was gradually pulled down, the stone reused for new building work. The most substantial part of the wall still standing is the western wall. Walk along its length and you can almost hear the skirl of bagpipes above the traffic. Or Northumbrian Pipes, if you want to support the home team.

Address Stowell Street, Newcastle, NE1 4XQ | **Getting there** Bus 131, 685, X 82 or X 85 to Newcastle St James (Stand D); Metro to St James (Yellow Line); paid parking at The Gate Car Park | **Tip** The only other substantial stretch of the town wall can be seen running parallel to Orchard Street, south of Newcastle Central Station.

107 __ William Jobling's Gibbet
Harsh but fair?

Our ancestors could never be accused of being soft on crime. Hanging was bad enough, but arguably worse was a punishment known as gibbeting. A gibbet was a body-shaped frame into which the corpse of an executed criminal could be placed. The gibbet would then be hung from gallows and left on public view as a deterrent to others. Often the corpse would be covered in tar to slow decomposition down, extending the time the body could be left to the elements. Horrifyingly, the criminal would sometimes still be alive when locked into the gibbet.

The practice of gibbeting ended in 1834 and the last person awarded this dubious honour was William Jobling, a miner from Jarrow. In 1832, there was a strike for better pay and conditions at the pit where Jobling worked. On the evening of 1 June, 1832, Jobling was walking back home from a night of drinking with Ralph Armstrong. The pair chanced upon Nicholas Fairles, a 71-year-old magistrate from South Shields. Short of money from the strike, Jobling and Armstrong asked Fairles for money. When Fairles refused, the two men began to beat him with sticks and stones.

Fairles survived long enough to describe the men to the authorities before dying from his injuries. Armstrong fled never to be heard of again, but Jobling was arrested and, after being found guilty, was hanged on 3 August watched by an excited crowd.

Jobling's remains were gibbeted at Jarrow Slake. His body was only on display for a few weeks before it mysteriously vanished one night. It is thought that his family were responsible, with his body buried in an unmarked grave. Although Jobling's body vanished, the gibbet was left intact. It is now on display in the South Shields Museum & Art Gallery. Inside the rusty frame of the gibbet is a replica of Jobling, his face understandably grim from the ordeal. But, it has to be said, he never broke another law afterwards.

Address Ocean Road, South Shields, NE33 2JA, +44 (0)191 211 5599, www.southshieldsmuseum.org.uk | **Getting there** Bus 1, 4, 10, 12, 516, 960, X 20 and various others to the South Shields Interchange; Metro to South Shields (Yellow Line); free parking at The Word Car Park for three hours and then a 10-minute walk | **Hours** Mon–Fri 11am–5pm, Sat 11am–4pm | **Tip** Ocean Beach Pleasure Park on the South Shields coast is the ideal place to dispel dark thoughts of Georgian crime. There are activities all year round, from a fun fair during the summer months to a festive light display in winter (Sea Road, South Shields, NE33 2LD, www.oceanbeach.co.uk).

108 The Windy Nook

Where a bridge came to rest

Newcastle and Gateshead, divided by the River Tyne, rely on bridges to allow the easy movement of both transport and pedestrians. Some of these bridges have become iconic symbols of Tyneside. Others have been washed away in floods or unceremoniously torn down and forgotten about. Only one bridge was carefully disassembled and its constituent parts placed at the top of a hill.

The current Scotswood Bridge opened to traffic in March 1967, replacing a suspension bridge built in 1831. The old bridge ultimately proved too small for the amount of traffic that crossed the Tyne, even in the comparatively less frenetic 1960s. Most of the steel from the suspension cables was salvaged, but that left the problem of what to do with the dressed granite blocks from the bridge's two towers.

Far from the river, the village of Windy Nook near Gateshead was once a place of industry, the men either working in nearby sandstone quarries or down one of south Tyneside's many collieries. By the 1980s, much of this industry was in decline or had disappeared completely. One unsightly remnant of Windy Nook's industrial past was a former colliery slag heap on the edge of the village. Enter the artist Richard Cole. His plan, in cooperation with Gateshead Council, was to transform the site into a huge environmental sculpture. The result, *The Windy Nook*, was unveiled in 1986 during Gateshead Sculpture Week.

Covering almost 6,000 square feet, *The Windy Nook* is a series of stone walls and earthworks that wrap around the hill on which it stands. In an inspired example of lateral thinking, the stone used by Coles was those left-over blocks from the old Scotswood Bridge, over 2,500 tons of them. In the decades since, the hill has naturalised. So successful has the transformation been that you could mistake *The Windy Nook* for a hill fort built by ancient Britons long before historical records began.

Address Off Whitehill Drive, Windy Nook | Getting there Bus 57 CityLink to Whitehill Drive–Dykesway; free parking off Whitehill Drive | Tip Nearby Windy Nook Nature Park is another example of wasteland turned to alternative use, offering pleasant walks across acid-heath grassland and through scrub woodland.

109 __ The Wooden Dolly

Shiver me timbers

North Shields, close to the mouth of the Tyne and the North Sea beyond, has a long nautical history. This history is made real in the form of wooden dollies, life-sized figures that have been on public show since the early 19th century.

The first wooden dolly was originally a figurehead taken from the *Alexander and Margaret*, a collier brig named after her owners. In 1815, she was placed at the entrance of Custom House Quay, a memorial to David Bartleman, Alexander and Margaret's son, who was mortally wounded on the brig during a skirmish with pirates in 1781.

Unfortunately for the dolly, sailors took to paring off slivers of wood from her face to keep as good luck charms on their voyages. She was also resented by locals as she prevented carts from entering the Quay. One day, in an act of frustration, ropes were tied around her ankles and she was used to haul heavy ships' masts up from the Quay, badly damaging her. Disfigured and a bit shabby, she suffered the final indignity of being toppled over and destroyed by drunks in 1850.

The first replacement was erected in 1850, and then a second followed in 1864. This dolly lost her nose to sailors, so a new nose of iron was made by a local blacksmith. In response, sailors started nailing coins to her body in order to ensure good luck. In 1902, a third replacement was carved by Miss Mary Spence, and paid for with local donations to celebrate the coronation of Edward VII. This dolly bucked tradition by representing a North Shields fisherwoman, carrying a creel of fish. She stood at the entrance of Custom House Quay until 1957.

For 35 years there was a dolly-shaped gap until the current wooden dolly was erected in the same spot in 1992. Made from solid oak, she was carved by the sculptors Martyn and Jane Grubb. Fortunately for her shapely face, the tradition of chopping off a nasal good luck charm is now discouraged.

Address Prince of Wales Tavern, Liddell Street, North Shields, NE30 1HE | Getting there Bus 333 to Liddell Street; free parking at Low Lights Car Park and then a 10-minute walk along Union Road/Bell Street | Tip A second wooden dolly, created by Robert 'Mouseman' Thompson, can also be seen in nearby Northumberland Square.

110_ The Word

In the beginning was the word

The Word, more formally known as the National Centre for the Written Word, is a new £100- million state-of-the-art facility right at the heart of South Shields. Across four floors, the written word is celebrated in all its glory, whether printed in a book or glowing on a computer screen.

It is fitting that South Shields is home to The Word. In 1906, Catherine Cookson, one of the most successful British authors of the 20th century, was born at 5 Leam Lane, near the Tyne Dock. The young Catherine 'Katie' McMullen, as she was then, grew up in extreme poverty. Life for working-class families on South Tyneside was hard in the early 1900s, with unemployment an escalating problem. Katie's family were Irish Catholics, immigrants who had moved to England in the 1840s after the potato famine. John McMullen, her hard-drinking step-grandfather, who, along with Rose, her grandmother, raised Katie. John had a reputation as a man to steer clear of.

What saved Katie was a love of reading, in particular a book of correspondence between the Earl of Chesterfield, an 18th-century Whig politician, and his son. This opened her eyes to a world beyond her immediate surroundings. In 1945, after moving to Hastings and marrying Tom Cookson, a teacher at a local grammar school, she joined the Hastings Writers' Circle. There she began to write a fictionalised account of her childhood experiences. The result was her first book, *Kate Hannigan*. Between this debut and her death in 1998, Cookson wrote more than 100 books, selling over 123 million copies worldwide. For a run of 17 years, Cookson was also the most borrowed author from public libraries in the United Kingdom, only dropping from first place four years after her death. Visit the extensive library in The Word and you can still borrow the books of Catherine Cookson, just 20 minutes' walk from the area that originally inspired them.

Address The Word, 45 Market Place, South Shields, NE33 1JF, +44 (0)191 427 1818, theworduk.org | **Getting there** Various to Church Way Bus and Coach Station; Metro to South Shields (Yellow Line), then a 10-minute walk; limited free parking at The Word Car Park | **Hours** Mon–Thu 9am–7pm, Fri 9am–5pm, Sat & Sun 10am–4pm | **Tip** North and South Marine Parks, a 20-minute walk from The Word, are pleasant open areas suitable for families. Facilities include play areas, a boating lake and a seasonal miniature steam railway.

111 The Wren Stone
The Portland Bill

In a corner of Newcastle Civic Centre's inner courtyard a rough-hewn stone has been carefully embedded in a wall. It is known as the Wren Stone and it links the Baroque splendour of St Paul's Cathedral in London with this cheerfully modernist local government building.

Sir Christopher Wren was the architect charged with the rebuilding of London after the Great Fire of 1666. One of his many, many tasks was the replacement of the medieval St Paul's Cathedral, which had been consumed by the conflagration. The material Wren chose to build the new church was Portland Stone, an off-white limestone from the late Jurassic period and found on the Isle of Portland off the Dorset coast. It is prized as a building material for the ease with which it can be worked, as well as its resistance to weathering. Happily, the stone also glows brilliantly in the right light, a side effect of its pale colouration. Wren took a personal interest in the stone quarried to build his masterpiece. Each block was checked by the architect and, if satisfied with its quality, he would add his 'signature' as a sign of approval.

During the planning stage of the Civic Centre, the decision was made to use Portland Stone for the exterior, making a bold visual statement in a city of buff sandstone and sober brick. Designed by City Architect George Kenyon, the building was completed in 1967 at a total cost of £4,855,000. The Portland Stone used for the Civic Centre came from the same quarry as that used for St Paul's. Tucked away in a corner of the quarry was a stone to which Wren had added his mark but curiously never had shipped to London. The owners of the quarry donated this stone to Newcastle in gratitude for the city's use of their product. So now the Civic Centre sports the stone, originally designed for a different building entirely and forgotten about for nearly 300 years.

THE WREN STONE

his stone was taken from one of the original quarried blocks personally selected at
ortland by Sir Christopher Wren for the rebuilding of St. Pauls Cathedral 1675-1710 & bears
is insignia of approval. It lay untouched in the quarries until it was presented to the City
1965 by The Stone Firms in recognition of the use of Portland Stone in this building

Address Newcastle Civic Centre, Newcastle, NE1 8QH | Getting there Bus 10, 43/44/45
Sapphire, 46, 47, X 14, X 30 and various others to Haymarket Barras Bridge; Metro to
Haymarket (Yellow or Green Line); paid parking at Sandyford Square (Civic Centre)
Car Park | Tip The Valley Junction is an Indian restaurant with a difference. Diners can
enjoy their meals either in a disused signal box or in an elegant railway carriage built in
1912 (The Old Station, Jesmond Three Sixty, Newcastle, NE2 1DB, +44 (0)191 281 6397,
www.valleyrestaurants.co.uk).

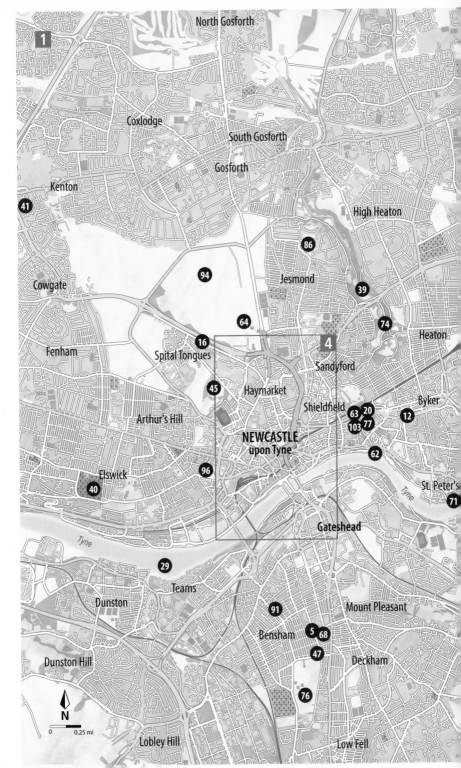

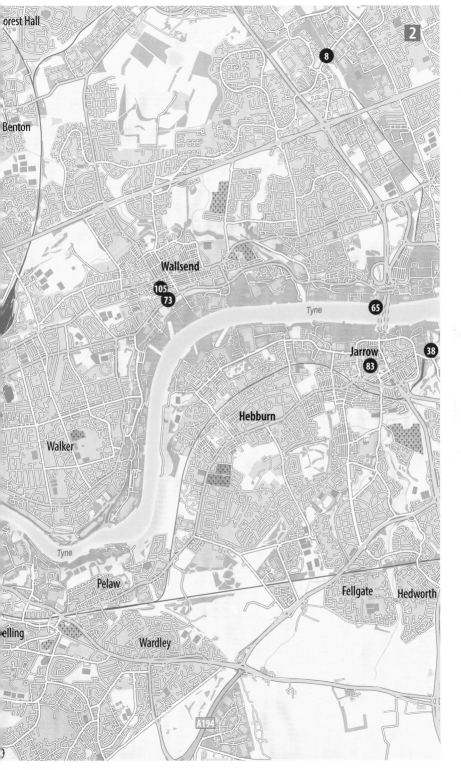

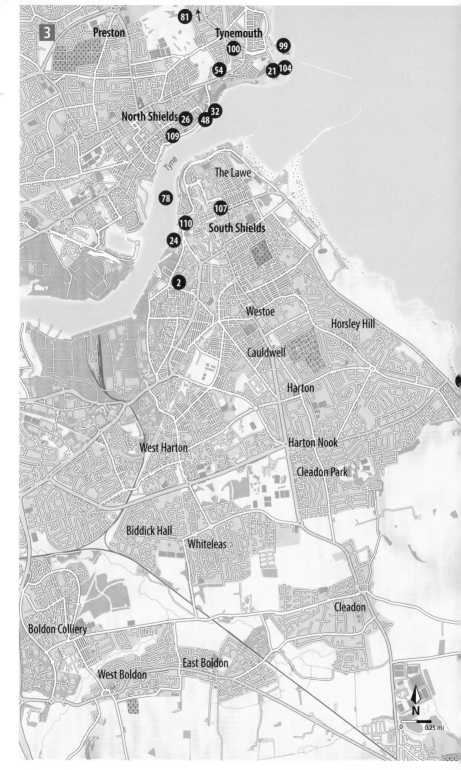

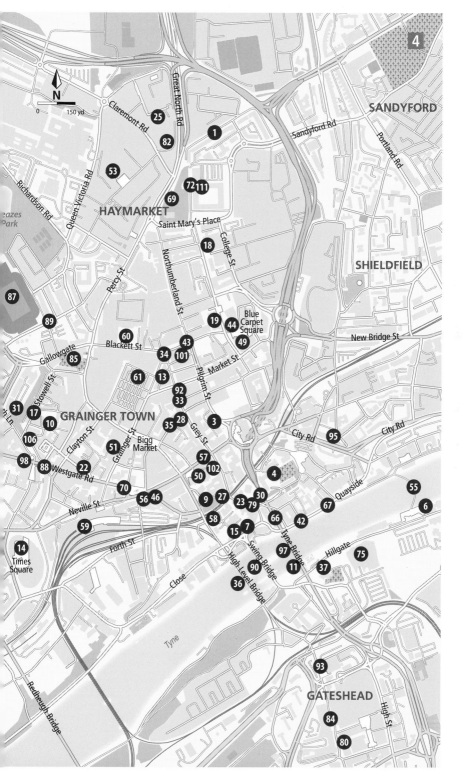

Solange Berchemin
111 Places in the Lake District
That You Shouldn't Miss
ISBN 978-3-7408-0378-0

Rob Ganley, Ian Williams
111 Places in Coventry
That You Shouldn't Miss
ISBN 978-3-7408-1044-3

Martin Booth, Barbara Evripidou
111 Places in Bristol
That You Shouldn't Miss
ISBN 978-3-7408-0898-3

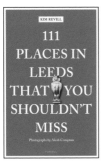

Kim Revill, Alesh Compton
111 Places in Leeds
That You Shouldn't Miss
ISBN 978-3-7408-0754-2

John Sykes, Birgit Weber
111 Places in London
That You Shouldn't Miss
ISBN 978-3-95451-346-8

Nicola Perry, Daniel Reiter
33 Walks in London
That You Shouldn't Miss
ISBN 978-3-95451-886-9

Kirstin von Glasow
111 Gardens in London
That You Shouldn't Miss
ISBN 978-3-7408-0143-4

Laura Richards, Jamie Newson
111 London Pubs and Bars
That You Shouldn't Miss
ISBN 978-3-7408-0893-8

Emma Rose Barber,
Benedict Flett
111 Churches in London
That You Shouldn't Miss
ISBN 978-3-7408-0901-0

Ed Glinert, Marc Zakian
**111 Places in London's East
End That You Shouldn't Miss**
ISBN 978-3-7408-0752-8

Julian Treuherz,
Peter de Figueiredo
**111 Places in Manchester
That You Shouldn't Miss**
ISBN 978-3-7408-0753-5

Julian Treuherz,
Peter de Figueiredo
**111 Places in Liverpool
That You Shouldn't Miss**
ISBN 978-3-95451-769-5

Michael Glover,
Richard Anderson
**111 Places in Sheffield
That You Shouldn't Miss**
ISBN 978-3-7408-0022-2

Katherine Bebo, Oliver Smith
**111 Places in Poole
That You Shouldn't Miss**
ISBN 978-3-7408-0598-2

Alexandra Loske
**111 Places in Brighton and
Lewes That You Shouldn't Miss**
ISBN 978-3-7408-0255-4

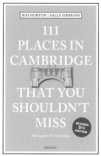

Rosalind Horton,
Sally Simmons, Guy Snape
**111 Places in Cambridge
That You Shouldn't Miss**
ISBN 978-3-7408-0147-2

Justin Postlethwaite
**111 Places in Bath
That You Shouldn't Miss**
ISBN 978-3-7408-0146-5

Gillian Tait
**111 Places in Edinburgh
That You Shouldn't Miss**
ISBN 978-3-95451-883-8

Tom Shields, Gillian Tait
111 Places in Glasgow
That You Shouldn't Miss
ISBN 978-3-7408-0256-1

Gillian Tait
111 Places in Fife
That You Shouldn't Miss
ISBN 978-3-7408-0597-5

Laszlo Trankovits
111 Places in Jerusalem
That You Shouldn't Miss
ISBN 978-3-7408-0320-9

Andrea Livnat,
Angelika Baumgartner
111 Places in Tel Aviv
That You Shouldn't Miss
ISBN 978-3-7408-0263-9

Alexia Amvrazi,
Diana Farr Louis, Diane Shugart,
Yannis Varouhakis
111 Places in Athens
That You Shouldn't Miss
ISBN 978-3-7408-0377-3

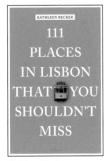

Kathleen Becker
111 Places in Lisbon
That You Shouldn't Miss
ISBN 978-3-7408-0383-4

Catrin George Ponciano
111 Places along the Algarve
That You Shouldn't Miss
ISBN 978-3-7408-0381-0

Thomas Fuchs
111 Places in Amsterdam
That You Shouldn't Miss
ISBN 978-3-7408-0023-9

Sybil Canac, Renée Grimaud,
Katia Thomas
111 Places in Paris
That You Shouldn't Miss
ISBN 978-3-7408-0159-5

For all their help during the writing of this book thank you to Alison at Bede Museum, Anne Marcantonio, Clive Goodwin, Emily Wright, Genny Silvanus, Hannah at Cake Stories, Hannah Evans, Ivan Lazarov, Jonathan Richards, Kay Easson at the Lit & Phil, Kate Sussams, Leann Hay, Lena Moss, Marsha at the Pink Lane Bakery, Mick at The Cluny, Mitch Mitchell, Phil Roughley at Newcastle University, the Acle Early Medieval Re-enactment Society, and Sandra Ellis. Special thanks go to Alistair Layzell for his patience, Karen Seiger and Laura Olk at Emons, and Ros Horton who edited the text. Also a thank you to my parents, Bill and Carol Taylor for their unceasing support. Jim and Sheilah for their friendship. And – last but far from least – thank you to my wife Tania, without whom I couldn't have written this book.

David Taylor was born in Newcastle and is a professional freelance landscape photographer and writer who now lives in Northumberland. David has written nearly 40 books about photography, as well as supplying images and articles to both regional and national magazines. When David is not outdoors he can be found at home with his wife, a cat, and a worryingly large number of tripods.